TOEIC®テスト
これだけ 直前1カ月
600点クリア

How to Prepare for the TOEIC® Test : Advanced Course

鹿野晴夫

研究社

Copyright © 2011 by ICC

『TOEIC®テスト　これだけ　直前1カ月　600点クリア』

PRINTED IN JAPAN

はじめに

▶ 本書を手にされたみなさんへ

　本書『TOEIC® テスト　これだけ　直前１カ月　600点クリア』を手に取っていただき、誠にありがとうございます。
　ところで、みなさんが本書を手にされた理由は何でしょうか？　その理由が下記のものであれば、まさに本書はお探しの本です。

① TOEIC スコアで、600点を超えたい
② TOEIC テスト受験までの１カ月間で、成果を出したい
③ 通勤・通学など、移動時間を有効に使いたい

　TOEIC テストに受験申し込みをしたあと、試験までの１カ月間に何をするか？　これがポイントです。多くの方は、TOEIC テストの問題集で学習を始めます。確かに TOEIC テストは、Part 1～ Part 7に分かれていて、問題形式がそれぞれ異なりますから、それに慣れていないと、高いスコアは望めません。
　ですので、テスト前に問題形式に慣れておくことは絶対に必要です。でも、試験までの１カ月間、ただ漠然と問題集を解くだけでは、実力アップは望めません。問題を解くだけでなく、復習が必要なのです。
　しかし、１カ月間でどれほどの復習ができるでしょうか？
　１日平均３時間、月100時間以上学習できる方は別として、満足に復習できないまま、試験当日を迎えてしまう方も少なくないでしょう。本書『TOEIC® テスト　これだけ　直前１カ月　600点クリア』は、通勤・通学の時間くらいしか使えない方も、問題形式に慣れるだけでなく、実力アップがはかれるように、工夫しました。本書には、次の特長があります。

① 300点台から出発した著者のノウハウを凝縮

　私のTOEICテスト初受験は、社会人29歳の時、スコアは335点でした。最初の頃は、「600点クリア」は高い目標でした。そこから、1年で610点、2年3カ月で760点、3年半で850点になりました。900点突破には、7年かかりましたが、初受験からのスコアアップは、600点以上です。

　TOEICスコアは、470点・600点・730点と、壁を超えるように伸びていきます。「600点の壁」は、すごく高い壁ではなさそうですが、そんなことはありません。事実、企業・学校内で実施されているTOEIC IPテストの結果では、600点未満の方が80%以上を占めています。

　なぜ600点をクリアできない方が多いのでしょう？　それは、「どうやって学習したらいいかわからない」という人が多いからです。本書は、久々に英語を学習する方も、迷わず1カ月間トレーニングできるように、工夫しています。

② 1カ月間で、問題形式に慣れるだけでなく、実力アップ

　TOEICテストが測る英語力は、「スピード対応能力」です。具体的には、「速い英語が聴ける」「意味の通じる語句をすぐに選べる」「速く読める」ということです。本書は、みなさんがTOEICの問題形式に慣れつつ、このスピード対応能力も同時にアップできるように計算のうえ、編纂しました。

③ テキストで学習し、音声CDで復習できる

　クイズ形式で練習問題を解き、解答・解説を確認したあと、音声CDを利用して、通学・通勤などのあいだに効果的に学習できるように工夫しました。

　みなさんが、本書を上手に活用し、TOEICテスト受験までの1カ月間の学習を効果的に進めていただけることを願っています。

2011年3月

鹿野 晴夫

『TOEIC® テスト これだけ 直前1カ月 600点クリア』

目次

はじめに …………………………………………………………………… 3

第1章　直前1カ月でも差がつくトレーニング法 ……………… 7

第2章　Week 1 ……………………………………………………… 13

第3章　Week 2 ……………………………………………………… 49

第4章　Week 3 ……………………………………………………… 85

第5章　Week 4 ……………………………………………………… 121

第6章　最終チェック ……………………………………………… 157

効果的に学習できるように、各レッスンの CD トラック番号は前から振っていないのでご注意ください（12 ページをご覧ください）。
　各レッスンの最初のトラックで Week 1 Day 1, Week 1 Day 2, Week 1 Day 3... とナレーションが入りますが、このトラック番号は記してありません。

第1章

直前1カ月でも差がつくトレーニング法

1. 学習の進め方

❶ 600点クリアに必要な力を理解する

　まず、TOEICテストで600点をクリアする正答目標を確認しましょう。正答目標には、偶然に正解するものを含みます。TOEICテストは、Part 2が3択、他のパートは4択ですから、ただ勘で解答用紙にマークしても、Part 2は33％、他のパートは25％の確率で正答します。

　出題数が多く、正答目標の高いパートは、Part 2, Part 5, Part 7のシングルパッセージです。3つの合計は98問で、そのうち69問が正答目標です。ですから、TOEICテスト受験まで1カ月を切ったら、迷わずこの3つのパートのスコアアップをめざして、トレーニングを行ないましょう。

　一方、出題数の多くないパート（Part 1, Part 6）、正答目標の高くないパート（Part 3, Part 4, Part 7のダブルパッセージ）については、問題形式に慣れることをまず考えましょう。

600点クリアのための正答目標

セクション	Part	形式	問題数	正答目標
リスニング 100問 （45分間）	1	写真描写問題	10問	80％
	2	応答問題	30問	70％
	3	会話問題	30問	50％
	4	説明文問題	30問	50％
リーディング 100問 （75分間）	5	短文穴埋め問題	40問	70％
	6	長文穴埋め問題	12問	65％
	7	読解問題（シングルパッセージ）	28問	70％
		読解問題（ダブルパッセージ）	20問	45％

2 1カ月間の学習の流れ

本書を活用したTOEICテスト受験前1カ月間の学習の流れは、以下のとおりです。第2章〜第5章の4章を1週間に1章のペースで進めて、受験直前に第6章を学習して、最終チェックをします。また、本書付属のCDを通勤・通学などのあいだに聞くことで、復習も効果的にできます。

章	週	テキスト学習内容	音声CD
第2章	Week 1	Day 1 説明文トレーニング	移動時間を活用して音声CDで復習
		Day 2 会話文トレーニング	
		Day 3 説明文トレーニング	
		Day 4 会話文トレーニング	
		Day 5 説明文トレーニング	
		Day 6 チェックテスト	
第3章	Week 2	Week 1同様	
第4章	Week 3		
第5章	Week 4		
第6章	受験直前	問題形式の最終チェック	

3 会話文・説明文トレーニングの英文

会話文トレーニングの英文は、Part 2（応答問題）の形式に近い問題を3問組み合わせました。Part 2は、話し手Aの短い問いかけに、話し手Bが発する4つの回答から最適なものを選ぶ問題です。本番のTOEICでは1問ずつすべて状況が異なりますが、これだと場面や状況といった周辺情報がなく、記憶に残りません。そこで本書では同じ状況を背景にした問題を3問組み合わせて、効果的にトレーニングできるようにしました。

説明文トレーニングの英文は、Part 7（読解問題）の形式に近い英文です。会話文・説明文ともに、TOEICテストで出題される日常生活とビジネスに関する話題を扱っています。リスニング・リーディング・文法・語彙を同じ英文でトレーニングすることで、音と文字の両面からスピード対応能力が強化でき、文法・語彙も自然と身に付きます。

2. トレーニングの方法

❶ 会話文・説明文トレーニングのステップ

　本書でメインとなる第2章～第4章の Day 1～ Day 5 のトレーニングです。トレーニングは、以下の Step 1～6 の順で、1回のトレーニング時間は約20～40分です。

Step	内容	目的	時間
1	リスニング問題 (Part 3, 4 形式 3 問)	Part 3, 4 の問題形式に慣れ、 Part 2 の正答数アップをめざす。	2分
2	リーディング問題 (Part 7 形式 3 問)	Part 7 の問題形式に慣れ、 Part 7 の正答数アップをめざす。	3分
3	文法・語彙問題 (Part 5 形式 5 問)	Part 5 の問題形式に慣れ、 Part 5 の正答数アップをめざす。	2分
4	解答・解説チェック	解答・解説をチェックし、現時点での理解度を確認する。	3分
5	直読直解トレーニング	直読直解トレーニングで、リスニング・リーディング力を伸ばす。	5～ 15分
6	基本構文トレーニング	基本構文トレーニングで、文法・語彙力を伸ばす。	5～ 15分

❷ 直読直解トレーニングの方法 ＜基本編＞

　TOEIC テストでは、ナチュラルスピード（1分間に150語以上）の英文を聞き、リーディング問題を最後まで解くには1分間に150語以上読まなければなりません。速読速聴が、まず求められます。1分間に150語以上「聞いて・読む」ことができれば、TOEIC 600点以上のスコアが期待できます。ですから、そのためには、うしろから訳して考えることなく、英語の語順どおりに理解し

ましょう。その練習が、「直読直解トレーニング」です。
　直読直解トレーニングの英文は、意味の区切りにスラッシュ（／）が入れてあり、意味の区切りごとに日本語訳を付けました。この英文を使って、区切り単位で、意味を理解する練習を行ないます。

直読直解トレーニング	1	CD（英語）を聞いて、英文を目で追う。
	2	CD（英語）を聞いて、日本語訳を目で追う。
	3	カンマ (,)、ピリオド (.)、スラッシュ (/) の単位で、英文の意味が理解できるか確認（理解できない部分は、日本語訳や語彙を参照）。

3 基本構文トレーニングの方法 ＜基本編＞

　TOEICテストには、空欄補充問題（Part 5, 6）もあります。文法・語彙問題ですが、30秒で解かないと、読解問題（Part 7）をやり残してしまいます。これは、「話す力」や「書く力」に通じるスピード対応能力を測る問題です。この能力を養うために、練習問題を解いたあと、問われていた文法・語彙を含んだ英文（基本構文）を使って、「基本構文トレーニング」を行ないます。
　われわれが母国語（日本語）を文法や語彙の理屈を意識しないで使えるのはどうしてでしょう？　それは、「リクツ」を考えなくても使えてしまう「リズム」を身に付けているからです。このリズムを身に付けるには、音読がいちばん。小学校の頃、毎日音読したのと一緒です。なお、電車の中などでは、小声か実際に声を出さない「口パク」でも効果があります。

基本構文トレーニング	1	1文ずつCD（日本語・英語）を聞き、英語を数回音読。
	2	10文の英語を続けて音読（数回）。
	3	テキストを縦に半分に折り、英語部分を見て意味がすぐにわかるか確認。

4 チェックテスト

　第2章～第4章のDay 6では、「チェックテスト」を行ないます。ここで、

Day 1〜Day 5で登場した単語50個の意味を確認します。Day 1〜Day 5のトレーニングの段階で、出てきた単語を意識して覚える必要はありません。Day 6のチェックテストで間違った単語の意味を確認し、通勤、通学の時間などを使って付属のCDでその音を聞けば、自然とインプットされるはずです。

5 第6章「最終チェック」

TOEICテストの問題形式を確認する25問の練習問題（約15分）です。第2章〜第5章のトレーニングを終えて、TOEICテスト受験直前に、問題形式の最終確認をして、本番に備えてください。

6 付属CDの活用方法

付属の音声CDは、下記のように構成されています。意識せずに、聞き流すだけで、語彙・基本構文の復習ができます。繰り返し聞きましょう。

CD音声が流れる順	収録	例
1	語句（日→英）	正気でない→ crazy
2	基本構文（日→英）	人は、運転中に信じられないことをします。People do some crazy things while driving.
3	本文（英）	People do some crazy things while driving: applying makeup, watching TV,
	設問（英）	1. Who is the speaker talking to?

（※効果的に学習できるように、各レッスンのCDトラック番号は前から順に振っていません。ご注意ください。）

何度も聞いて英文になじんできたら、発音された単語を続いて言ってみる（crazyのあとで、crazyと発音する）、基本構文の日本語を聞いたあと、英語の部分でシャドウイングしてみたり（少し遅れて、声をかぶせるようにつぶやく）、設問のあとでテキストを見ずに答えを考えるなどすれば、さらに効果的です。

第 2 章

Week 1

Week 1
今週のトレーニング

	Day 1〜 Day 5 のトレーニング		
Step	内容		時間
1	リスニング問題（3問）		2分
2	リーディング問題（3問）		3分
3	文法・語彙問題（5問）		2分
4	解答・解説チェック		3分
5	直読直解トレーニング		5〜15分
	①	CD（英語）を聞いて、英文を目で追う。	
	②	CD（英語）を聞いて、日本語訳を目で追う。	
	③	カンマ（,）、ピリオド（.）、スラッシュ（/）の単位で、英文の意味が理解できるか確認（理解できない部分は、日本語訳や語彙を参照）。	
6	基本構文トレーニング		5〜15分
	①	1文ずつCD（日本語・英語）を聞き、英語を数回音読。	
	②	10文の英語を続けて音読（数回行なう）。	
	③	テキストを縦に半分に折るなどして日本語訳を隠し、英語部分を見て意味がすぐにわかるか確認。	

＜ワンポイント＞

　まず、上記の基本的な手順に沿ってトレーニングしてください。Step 1「リスニング問題」がむずかしく感じられるかもしれません。これは、TOEIC Part 3, 4形式の問題ですから、むずかしく感じて当然です。8ページで説明したように、Part 3, 4は形式に慣れておくことが目的です。「むずかしく感じて当然」くらいの気持ちで、割り切ってトライしてください。問題が解けなくても、落ち込む必要はありません。手順に沿ってトレーニングすれば、確実に実力アップします。今日より、明日の自分の変化を信じて、がんばりましょう。

Day 1 説明文トレーニング

Step 1 リスニング問題
CDを聞いて、問題を解こう。＜制限時間2分＞

Q1. What is the purpose of the announcement?
　　(A) To request information
　　(B) To give news
　　(C) To report on local weather
　　(D) To criticize local traffic authorities

Q2. What could cause listeners problems?
　　(A) Flooding near exits 344 and 346
　　(B) The current weather situation
　　(C) Chopper 9
　　(D) Some accidents

Q3. When was the announcement made?
　　(A) Before noon
　　(B) At noon exactly
　　(C) In late afternoon
　　(D) In early evening

Step 2　リーディング問題

英文を読んで、問題を解こう。＜制限時間3分＞

Traffic is backed up on the 405 this morning as we have two accidents to report. One is at exit 320 to Mason Way involving an SUV and a large flatbed truck. The other is a fender-bender in the right lane, southbound, between exits 344 and 346. The police are on the scene at both locations, and traffic, although slow, is moving now. Other than that, the bridges seem clear. Traffic through the tunnel, although backed up a little, is moving fairly rapidly. That's your traffic report for this hour. I'm Carol Stahl. I'll be back at about 20 past the hour, next hour, reporting from Chopper 9.

Q4.　What are 320, 344, 346, and 405?
　　　(A) They are numbers of highways.
　　　(B) They are numbers given to accidents.
　　　(C) They all are numbers of exits on a major highway.
　　　(D) The last one is a highway number; the others are exit numbers.

Q5.　Where is Carol Stahl?
　　　(A) In the air
　　　(B) In a studio
　　　(C) On a highway
　　　(D) At the scene of an accident

Q6.　If this report was made at 7:50 a.m., when will the next one be made?
　　　(A) At 8:00 a.m.
　　　(B) At about 8:20 a.m.
　　　(C) At about 8:40 a.m.
　　　(D) At about 8:50 a.m.

Step 3　文法・語彙問題
空欄にふさわしい語句を選ぼう。＜制限時間2分＞

Q7. Please note that traffic is backed ----- on the 405.
　　(A) in
　　(B) off
　　(C) up
　　(D) out

Q8. We know that the police are on the ----- at both locations.
　　(A) scenic
　　(B) scene
　　(C) scenery
　　(D) scenically

Q9. I'll be ----- at about 20 past the hour with the next report.
　　(A) back
　　(B) again
　　(C) returned
　　(D) once more

Q10. The other is a ----- in the right lane of Highway 441.
　　(A) bender-fender
　　(B) fender-bender
　　(C) bender-to-fender
　　(D) fender-to-bender

Q11. Traffic through the tunnel is moving ----- rapidly.
　　(A) fair
　　(B) fare
　　(C) fairly
　　(D) fairy

Step 4　解答・解説チェック

現時点での理解度を確認しよう。

問題文は、朝の道路交通情報を伝えるアナウンスです。

1. 正解 **(B)**。質問:「このお知らせの目的は、何ですか？」。答え:「ニュースを知らせる」。ヒント:話の内容全体から。
2. 正解 **(D)**。質問:「聞き手に起こりうる問題の原因は、何ですか？」。答え:「ある種の事故」。ヒント:Traffic is backed up ... as we have two accidents to report.
3. 正解 **(A)**。質問:「このお知らせが行なわれたのは、いつですか？」。答え:「午前中」。ヒント:Traffic is backed up on the 405 this morning
4. 正解 **(D)**。質問:「320、344、346 と 405 は、何ですか？」。答え:「最後はハイウェイ番号で、他は出口番号」。ヒント:Traffic is backed up on the 405, exit 320, exits 344 and 346
5. 正解 **(A)**。質問:「キャロル・ストールはどこにいますか？」。答え:「空中」。ヒント:reporting from Chopper 9
6. 正解 **(B)**。質問:「このレポートが行なわれたのが 7 時 50 分なら、次のレポートが行なわれるのはいつですか？」。答え:「午前 8 時 20 分頃」。ヒント:I'll be back at about 20 past the hour, next hour
7. 正解 **(C)**。文意から、be backed up「渋滞している」の現在形を完成させる。
8. 正解 **(B)**。文意から、on the scene「現場に」を完成させる。
9. 正解 **(A)**。文意から、I'll be back「またのちほど」を完成させる。
10. 正解 **(B)**。文意から、fender-bender「（車同士の）接触事故」を選ぶ。
11. 正解 **(C)**。動詞 moving（現在分詞）と副詞 rapidly「迅速に」の間なので、副詞 fairly「比較的」を選ぶ。

Step 5　直読直解トレーニング

速読速聴力を高めよう。
（※日本語訳は、英語の原文の順序どおりに記してあります。）

Traffic is backed up / on the 405 / this morning / as we have two accidents /
車が渋滞しています、405号線で、今朝、2件の事故によるものです、
to report. One is at exit 320 / to Mason Way / involving an SUV /
お伝えする。1つは320番出口、メイソンウェイ方面への、SUVが関わった、
and a large flatbed truck. The other is / a fender-bender / in the right lane,
それと大型平床トラック。もう1つは、車両同士の接触事故です、右車線での、
southbound, between exits 344 and 346. The police are / on the scene /
南へ向かう、344番と346番出口の間での。警察は、到着しています、
at both locations, and traffic, although slow, is moving now.
どちらの現場にも、そして車は、ゆっくりですが、現在は流れています。
Other than that, the bridges seem clear. Traffic through the tunnel,
それ以外では、橋での渋滞はないようです。トンネル内の交通は、
although backed up a little, is moving fairly rapidly.
多少渋滞していますが、比較的順調に流れています。
That's your traffic report / for this hour. I'm Carol Stahl. I'll be back /
以上が、交通情報です、この時間の。キャロル・ストールです。またのちほど、
at about 20 past the hour, next hour, reporting from Chopper 9.
およそ20分過ぎ頃に、次の時報の、チョッパー9からレポートします。

語句			
be backed up：渋滞している		exit：出口	
involve：〜を巻き込む		flatbed：平床式の	
fender-bender：車同士の接触事故		on the scene：現場に	
location：場所		clear：渋滞していない	
the hour：正時		chopper：ヘリコプター	

Step 6　基本構文トレーニング

文法・語彙力を高めよう。

1	405号線で、車が渋滞しています。	Traffic is backed up on the 405.
2	2件の事故をお伝えします。	We have two accidents to report.
3	1つは、メイソンウェイ方面への320番出口です。	One is at exit 320 to Mason Way.
4	もう1つは、右車線で発生した車両同士の接触事故です。	The other is a fender-bender in the right lane.
5	どちらの現場にも、警察が到着しています。	The police are on the scene at both locations.
6	車は、ゆっくりですが、現在は流れています。	Traffic, although slow, is moving now.
7	それ以外では、橋での渋滞はないようです。	Other than that, the bridges seem clear.
8	トンネル内の交通は、比較的順調に流れています。	Traffic through the tunnel is moving fairly rapidly.
9	以上、この時間の交通情報でした。	That's your traffic report for this hour.
10	またのちほど、20分過ぎ頃に。	I'll be back at about 20 past the hour.

Day 2 会話文トレーニング

Step 1　リスニング問題

CDを聞いて、問題を解こう。＜制限時間2分＞

Q1.　Where are these people?
　　(A) On a fishing boat
　　(B) In a restaurant
　　(C) In an office
　　(D) On a subway

Q2.　Who are the speakers?
　　(A) Partners
　　(B) Businesspeople
　　(C) Fishermen
　　(D) Waiters

Q3.　What does the woman want to do next?
　　(A) Order dessert
　　(B) Sign a contract
　　(C) Get a refill
　　(D) Talk to her business partner

Step 2　リーディング問題

英文を読んで、問題を解こう。＜制限時間 3 分＞

M: I highly recommend the salmon fillet.
W: I'm not big on fish, though.

M: Now the way I see it, you need a higher-profile Web presence.
W: That is one step we want to take. I also like your idea on direct marketing.
M: Yes, I think that's the way to go. Oh, here's the waiter. Excuse me, could I get a refill, please?

M: Let's order some dessert, and afterwards we can head back to my office to sign the contracts.
W: Do you mind if we wait on that? I'd really like my partner to look over the contracts with me.

Q4. What does the woman say she does not like very much?
 (A) Direct marketing　　(B) Business
 (C) Dessert　　(D) Fish

Q5. What does the woman agree with the man about?
 (A) Going to his office
 (B) Using the Web more
 (C) Ordering the salmon fillet
 (D) Signing a contract after lunch

Q6. What does the conversation reveal about the woman?
 (A) She is not in business alone.
 (B) She is new in the world of business.
 (C) She and the man are business partners.
 (D) She is having problems in her business.

Step 3　文法・語彙問題
空欄にふさわしい語句を選ぼう。＜制限時間2分＞

Q7. That is one step we want ---- in the near future.
　　(A) taking
　　(B) to take
　　(C) have to take
　　(D) will have taken

Q8. I think that's ---- to go, because it will improve sales.
　　(A) away
　　(B) the ways
　　(C) always
　　(D) the way

Q9. We can ---- back to my office to sign the papers.
　　(A) foot
　　(B) leg
　　(C) head
　　(D) hand

Q10. I highly ---- the salmon fillet if you can't decide what to order.
　　(A) to recommend
　　(B) recommend
　　(C) recommendation
　　(D) recommending

Q11. I'd like my partner to ---- over the contracts before we sign anything.
　　(A) see
　　(B) watch
　　(C) study
　　(D) look

Step 4　解答・解説チェック

現時点での理解度を確認しよう。

問題文は、食事をしながら、ビジネスの展開について話している男女の会話です。

1. 正解 **(B)**。質問：「話し手たちは、どこにいますか？」。答え：「レストラン」。ヒント：I highly recommend the salmon fillet., Oh, here's the waiter., Let's order some dessert
2. 正解 **(B)**。質問：「話し手たちは、どんな人ですか？」。答え：「ビジネスピープル」。ヒント：I also like your idea on direct marketing., afterwards we can head back to my office to sign the contracts.
3. 正解 **(D)**。質問：「女性が次にしたいことは、何ですか？」。答え：「ビジネスパートナーと話をする」。ヒント：I'd really like my partner to look over the contracts with me.
4. 正解 **(D)**。質問：「女性が、あまり好きでないと言っているのは何ですか？」。答え：「魚」。ヒント：I'm not big on fish
5. 正解 **(B)**。質問：「女性は、何に関して男性に同意していますか？」。答え：「もっとウェブを利用すること」。ヒント：男性の you need a higher-profile Web presence, 女性の That is one step we want to take.
6. 正解 **(A)**。質問：「この会話から、女性についてわかることは何ですか？」。答え：「1人で事業を行なっているのではない」。ヒント：I'd really like my partner to look over the contracts with me.
7. 正解 **(B)**。to take を選び、want to + 動詞「〜したい」を完成させる。
8. 正解 **(D)**。文意から、that's the way to go「それが（正しい）やり方です」を完成させる。
9. 正解 **(C)**。文意から、head back to「〜に戻る」を完成させる。
10. 正解 **(B)**。副詞 highly「大いに」のあとなので、動詞 recommend を選ぶ。
11. 正解 **(D)**。文意から、look over「〜に目を通す」を選ぶ。

Step 5　直読直解トレーニング

速読速聴力を高めよう。

（※日本語訳は、英語の原文の順序どおりに記してあります。）

M: I highly recommend / the salmon fillet.
　　ぜひおすすめします、サーモンのフィレを。

W: I'm not big on fish, though.
　　でも、魚はあまり好みません。

M: Now / the way I see it, you need a higher-profile Web presence.
　　さて、私の見るところでは、もっとウェブ上で存在を示すことが必要です。

W: That is one step / we want to take.
　　それが1つの手段です、われわれが取りたい。
　　I also like your idea / on direct marketing.
　　あなたのアイデアも気に入ってます、直販に関する。

M: Yes, I think that's the way to go. Oh, here's the waiter.
　　そう、その方法がいいと思います。あ、ウエイターが来ました。
　　Excuse me, could I get a refill, please?
　　すみません、お代わりをお願いします。

M: Let's order some dessert, and afterwards /
　　デザートを頼みましょう、そしてそのあとで、
　　we can head back to my office / to sign the contracts.
　　私のオフィスに戻りましょう、契約書に署名するために。

W: Do you mind / if we wait on that?
　　よろしいですか、それについては少しお待ちいただいて？
　　I'd really like my partner / to look over the contracts / with me.
　　どうしても私のパートナーにほしいのです、契約書に目を通して、一緒に。

語句
highly：大いに　**fillet**：フィレ［切り身］　**big on**：〜が大好きで
profile：世間の認知　**presence**：存在　**direct marketing**：直販　**refill**：お代わり
afterwards：そのあとで　**contract**：契約書　**wait on**：〜を保留する

Step 6　基本構文トレーニング
文法・語彙力を高めよう。

11	サーモンのフィレを、ぜひおすすめします。	I highly recommend the salmon fillet.
12	でも、魚はあまり好みません。	I'm not big on fish, though.
13	もっとウェブ上で存在を示すことが必要です。	You need a higher-profile Web presence.
14	それが、われわれが取りたい1つの手段です。	That is one step we want to take.
15	直販に関するあなたのアイデアも気に入ってます。	I also like your idea on direct marketing.
16	その方法がいいと思います。	I think that's the way to go.
17	お代わりをお願いします。	Could I get a refill, please?
18	私のオフィスに戻りましょう。	We can head back to my office.
19	それについては、少しお待ちいただけませんか？	Do you mind if we wait on that?
20	私のパートナーに、契約書に目を通してほしいのです。	I'd like my partner to look over the contracts.

Week 1

Day 3   説明文トレーニング

Step 1   リスニング問題
CDを聞いて、問題を解こう。＜制限時間2分＞

Q1. How many sports are mentioned in the talk?
 (A) One
 (B) Two
 (C) Three
 (D) Four

Q2. What happened at the Under 17 Championships in Peru last year?
 (A) A new ball was used.
 (B) Peru won the tournament.
 (C) Instant replay was used for the first time ever.
 (D) Disputed rulings were completely eliminated.

Q3. Why is new technology being introduced in some sports?
 (A) To speed up slow sports
 (B) To help referees and umpires make better decisions
 (C) To help athletes avoid serious injuries
 (D) To teach fans the most complex rules of games

Step 2 リーディング問題

英文を読んで、問題を解こう。＜制限時間3分＞

Sports has often been slow to adopt technology that would help officials make rulings on the field of play. Instant replay has crept in slowly and seems to work well in some sports such as rugby and basketball. Soccer, on the other hand, has been tradition-bound until now. A new "smartball" was tested at the Under-17 Championships in Peru last year with some success. The new ball itself has a chip implanted in it. Sensors are located near the goal lines to detect whether the whole ball has crossed the line or not. Officials hope this will eliminate some disputed rulings.

Q4. According to the passage, what is true of technology in sports?
   (A) It is widely used now.
   (B) It is liked by most players.
   (C) It has been introduced slowly.
   (D) It is disliked by most sports officials.

Q5. How are rugby, basketball and soccer compared?
   (A) By their popularity
   (B) By their use of technology
   (C) By the numbers of players on teams
   (D) By the parts of the world where they are played

Q6. In what sport is a new kind of ball being used?
   (A) Soccer
   (B) Rugby
   (C) Basketball
   (D) American football

Step 3 文法・語彙問題
空欄にふさわしい語句を選ぼう。＜制限時間2分＞

Q7. Instant replay has crept ----- slowly and now is common on TV.
　　(A) on
　　(B) into
　　(C) in
　　(D) around

Q8. Soccer has been tradition-bound ----- now.
　　(A) by
　　(B) until
　　(C) after
　　(D) under

Q9. As part of the technology, sensors ----- near the goal lines.
　　(A) locate
　　(B) are locating
　　(C) are located
　　(D) will locate

Q10. Until recently, sports ----- often been slow to adopt technology.
　　(A) was
　　(B) has
　　(C) have
　　(D) had

Q11. A new "smartball" was tested with some ----- in recent years.
　　(A) successful
　　(B) succeed
　　(C) success
　　(D) succeeding

Step 4 解答・解説チェック

現時点での理解度を確認しよう。

問題文は、スポーツにおける技術の進歩についてです。

1. 正解 **(C)**。質問：「話の中で、何種類のスポーツが述べられていますか」。答え：「3 種類」。ヒント：such as rugby and basketball. Soccer, on the other hand
2. 正解 **(A)**。質問：「去年のペルーでのアンダー17 選手権で、何が起こりましたか？」。答え：「新しいボールが使われた」。ヒント：A new "smartball" was tested at the Under-17 Championships in Peru last year
3. 正解 **(B)**。質問：「なぜ、いくつかのスポーツで新しい技術が導入されているのですか？」。答え：「レフリーや審判が、よりよい判断を下せるように」。ヒント：Sports ... adopt technology that would help officials make rulings on the field of play. Instant replay has crept in ... in some sports
4. 正解 **(C)**。質問：「文書によると、スポーツにおける技術に関して正しいものはどれですか？」。答え：「徐々に導入されている」。ヒント：Sports has often been slow to adopt technology
5. 正解 **(B)**。質問：「ラグビー、バスケットボール、サッカーはどのように比較されていますか？」。答え：「技術の利用具合によって」。ヒント：全体の内容から。
6. 正解 **(A)**。質問：「新種のボールが使われているのは、どのスポーツですか？」。答え：「サッカー」。ヒント：Soccer, ... until now. A new "smartball" was tested
7. 正解 **(C)**。creep in「(いつのまにか)入り込む」の現在完了形を完成させる。
8. 正解 **(B)**。文意から、until now「現在まで (ずっと)」を完成させる。
9. 正解 **(C)**。センサーは、「設置されるもの」なので、are located (受動態) を選ぶ。
10. 正解 **(B)**。been があるので現在完了形にするために has を選ぶ。ここでの sports は、「スポーツ全体」を表わしているので単数扱い。
11. 正解 **(C)**。前置詞 with のあとには名詞 (相当語句) がくる。success「成功」(名詞) を選ぶ。

Step 5　直読直解トレーニング

速読速聴力を高めよう。

(※日本語訳は、英語の原文の順序どおりに記してあります。)

Sports has often been slow / to adopt technology / that would help /
スポーツはしばしば手間取ります、技術を取り入れることに、助けるであろう、
officials make rulings / on the field of play. Instant replay /
審判員が判定する、試合のフィールドで。その場でのビデオ再生が、
has crept in slowly / and seems to work well / in some sports /
徐々に取り入れられ、うまくいっているようです、いくつかのスポーツで、
such as rugby and basketball. Soccer, on the other hand,
ラグビーやバスケットボールといった。サッカーは、その一方で、
has been tradition-bound / until now. A new "smartball" was tested /
伝統にしばられたままです、これまで。新しい「スマートボール」が試みられ、
at the Under-17 Championships / in Peru last year / with some success.
U-17選手権で、昨年ペルーで開催の、まずまずの成功を収めました。
The new ball itself / has a chip implanted in it. Sensors are located /
新しいボールに、チップが埋め込まれています。センサーが設置されています、
near the goal lines / to detect whether / the whole ball /
ゴールライン付近に、〜を感知するために、ボールが完全に、
has crossed the line or not. Officials hope / this will eliminate /
ラインを越えたかどうか。審判員は期待しています、これがなくすことを、
some disputed rulings.
もめる判定を。

語句			
adopt：〜を採用する		**ruling**：判定	
instant：即座の		**creep in**：入り込む	
tradition-bound：伝統にしばられた		**implant**：〜をはめ込む	
detect：〜を検知する		**cross**：〜を横切る	
eliminate：〜を取り除く		**disputed**：争点となっている	

Step 6　基本構文トレーニング
文法・語彙力を高めよう。

21	スポーツは、技術を取り入れることにしばしば手間取っています。	Sports has often been slow to adopt technology.
22	それは、審判員が判定する助けになるでしょう。	It would help officials make rulings.
23	その場でのビデオ再生が徐々に取り入れられています。	Instant replay has crept in slowly.
24	それは、いくつかのスポーツで、うまくいっているようです。	That seems to work well in some sports.
25	サッカーは、これまで伝統にしばられたままです。	Soccer has been tradition-bound until now.
26	新しい「スマートボール」が試みられ、まずまずの成功を収めました。	A new "smartball" was tested with some success.
27	新しいボールには、チップが埋め込まれています。	The new ball has a chip implanted in it.
28	ゴールライン付近にセンサーが設置されています。	Sensors are located near the goal lines.
29	ボールが完全にラインを越えました。	The whole ball has crossed the line.
30	これで、もめる判定がなくなるでしょう。	This will eliminate some disputed rulings.

Day 4　会話文トレーニング

Step 1　リスニング問題
CDを聞いて、問題を解こう。＜制限時間2分＞

Q1. What is causing the woman a problem?
　　(A) Her husband
　　(B) Her car
　　(C) Her boss
　　(D) Her computer

Q2. What did the woman think of the man's advice?
　　(A) She thought it was confusing.
　　(B) She thought it was useful.
　　(C) She thought it was worthless.
　　(D) She thought it was disturbing.

Q3. How are the two people communicating?
　　(A) By letter
　　(B) In person
　　(C) By phone
　　(D) Through the Internet

Step 2　リーディング問題
英文を読んで、問題を解こう。＜制限時間3分＞

M:　MPL Tech Support. Dominick speaking. How may I help you?
W:　Well, it's my Internet connection.

M:　I think I know what the problem is.
W:　That's a relief. What could it be that's slowing down my connection speed?
M:　Well, my guess is it's your firewall, but we can change the settings a bit to speed things up. I'll walk you through it.

M:　OK, that should solve your problem. Give it a try.
W:　OK, just give me a second here to log on....OK, wow! That loaded fast. Looks like everything is fine. Thank you so much.

Q4.　Why has the woman called?
　　　(A) Her computer is broken.
　　　(B) She wants to buy some software.
　　　(C) She wants to pay for faster service.
　　　(D) Her Internet connection is too slow.

Q5.　What does the man tell the woman?
　　　(A) Her computer is too slow.
　　　(B) Her problem may be caused by her firewall.
　　　(C) Her computer should be replaced.
　　　(D) Her problem cannot be solved right away.

Q6.　How does the woman feel at the end of the conversation?
　　　(A) Worried　　　　　　　　(B) Confused
　　　(C) Relieved　　　　　　　 (D) Angry

Step 3 文法・語彙問題

空欄にふさわしい語句を選ぼう。＜制限時間2分＞

Q7. I was very worried about it, so that's a ----.
（A）relief
（B）relax
（C）freedom
（D）wonderful

Q8. My ---- is it's your firewall, although I'm not sure.
（A）guest
（B）guessing
（C）guessed
（D）guess

Q9. I'll walk you ---- it and you can make the changes.
（A）with
（B）in
（C）through
（D）on

Q10. What could be ---- down my connection speed?
（A）slow
（B）slowing
（C）to slow
（D）slowed

Q11. Just give me ---- here to log on and I'll see if it works.
（A）second
（B）the second
（C）a second
（D）sec

Step 4　解答・解説チェック
現時点での理解度を確認しよう。

問題文は、インターネットの接続速度が遅い、という問題を抱えた女性とサポート係の会話です。

1. 正解 **(D)**。質問：「女性の問題の原因になっているのは、何ですか？」。答え：「彼女のコンピュータ」。ヒント：Well, it's my Internet connection.
2. 正解 **(B)**。質問：「女性は、男性のアドバイスをどう思いましたか？」。答え：「役に立ったと考えた」。ヒント：Thank you so much.
3. 正解 **(C)**。質問：「2人は、どんな方法で会話していますか？」。答え：「電話で」。ヒント：MPL Tech Support. Dominick speaking.
4. 正解 **(D)**。質問：「女性は、なぜ電話をかけましたか？」。答え：「彼女のインターネットの接続が遅すぎるため」。ヒント：What could it be that's slowing down my connection speed?
5. 正解 **(B)**。質問：「男性は、女性に何を伝えましたか？」。答え：「彼女の問題は、おそらくファイアウォールが原因である」。ヒント：Well, my guess is it's your firewall,
6. 正解 **(C)**。質問：「会話の最後で、女性はどんな気分でしたか？」。答え：「ほっとした」。ヒント：Looks like everything is fine.
7. 正解 **(A)**。冠詞のあとなので、名詞がくる。relief を選び、That's a relief.「それを聞いてほっとした」を完成させる。
8. 正解 **(D)**。代名詞 my のあとなので、名詞がくる。guess を選び、my guess is「私の推測では」を完成させる。(B) は動名詞で、my guessing「私が想像（すること）」となり、文意に合わない。
9. 正解 **(C)**。through を選び、walk +（人）+ through +（物）「（人）に（物）を手取り足取り教える」を完成させる。
10. 正解 **(B)**。be 動詞のあとなので、slowing を選び、slow down「～を遅くする」の現在進行形を完成させる。
11. 正解 **(C)**。a second を選び、give me a second「少し待ってください」を完成させる。

Step 5　直読直解トレーニング

速読速聴力を高めよう。

（※日本語訳は、英語の原文の順序どおりに記してあります。）

M: MPL Tech Support. Dominick speaking. How may I help you?
　　MPLテックサポート。ドミニクです。ご用件は？
W: Well, it's my Internet connection.
　　ええと、インターネットの接続です。

M: I think / I know what the problem is.
　　私は思います、何が問題なのかわかったと。
W: That's a relief.
　　それはほっとしました。
　　What could it be that's slowing down / my connection speed?
　　遅くしているものは何なのでしょうか、接続速度を？
M: Well, my guess is / it's your firewall, but we can change the settings /
　　そうですね、推測では、ファイアウォールです、でも設定を変更できます、
　　a bit / to speed things up. I'll walk you through it.
　　多少、それらのスピードがアップするように。私がガイドします。

M: OK, that should solve your problem. Give it a try.
　　結構です、それであなたの問題は解決したはずです。試してみてください。
W: OK, just give me a second here to log on....OK, wow!
　　はい、ここで少し時間をください、ログオンするのに、はい、まあ！
　　That loaded fast. Looks like everything is fine. Thank you so much.
　　素早く読み込みました。すべて順調のようです。ありがとうございました。

語句
connection：接続　**relief**：安堵　**slow down**：～を遅くする　**guess**：推測
setting：設定　**a bit**：ほんの少し　**speed up**：～のスピードを上げる
walk someone through something：（人）に（物）を手取り足取り教える
solve：～を解決する　**load**：ロードする

Step 6 基本構文トレーニング

文法・語彙力を高めよう。

31	ドミニクです。	Dominick speaking.
32	問題が何なのかわかったと思います。	I think I know what the problem is.
33	それは、ほっとしました。	That's a relief.
34	何が接続速度を遅くしているのでしょう？	What could be slowing down my connection speed?
35	私の推測では、ファイアウォールです。	My guess is it's your firewall.
36	それらをスピードアップするよう設定を変更できます。	We can change the settings to speed things up.
37	私がガイドします。	I'll walk you through it.
38	それで問題は解決したはずです。	That should solve your problem.
39	試してみてください。	Give it a try.
40	ログオンするのに、ここで少し時間をください。	Just give me a second here to log on.

Day 5　説明文トレーニング

Step 1　リスニング問題
CDを聞いて、問題を解こう。＜制限時間2分＞

Q1. According to the talk, what do dogs do?
　　(A) Make people feel better
　　(B) Guard people's valuables
　　(C) Guide people through crowded places
　　(D) Teach people new skills

Q2. When did "Dogs for Seniors" begin?
　　(A) A few weeks back
　　(B) This year
　　(C) Two months ago
　　(D) The year before last

Q3. What does the speaker think of "Dogs for Seniors"?
　　(A) It causes some doubts.
　　(B) It is a failure.
　　(C) It is good.
　　(D) It is strange.

Step 2　リーディング問題
英文を読んで、問題を解こう。＜制限時間３分＞

A dog is man's best friend, as the old saying goes. Now there's a new kind of therapy which shows that it's certainly true for many elderly people who are homebound or are in nursing homes. Older people in these situations often get depressed. Now, dogs cannot replace human contact, but they can raise people's spirits and get them into a healthier frame of mind. The "therapy" dogs are brought around to private homes and nursing homes once or twice a week to allow residents to interact with these animals. This program is called "Dogs for Seniors," and after two years it has proven to be a runaway success.

Q4.　Who receives the therapy mentioned in the passage?
　　(A) Pets
　　(B) Nurses
　　(C) Older people
　　(D) Owners of pets

Q5.　What is said about some people living in nursing homes?
　　(A) They become depressed.
　　(B) They want to have pets.
　　(C) They do not have many friends.
　　(D) They are stay in bed because they are sick.

Q6.　How often do therapy dogs visit people?
　　(A) As often as possible
　　(B) Usually once a month
　　(C) Two or three times a week
　　(D) About four to eight times a month

Step 3 文法・語彙問題

空欄にふさわしい語句を選ぼう。＜制限時間2分＞

Q7. Dogs cannot ----- human contact, but they can raise people's spirits.
　　(A) redo
　　(B) reform
　　(C) remake
　　(D) replace

Q8. Dogs make people feel happy, and they can get them into a healthier frame of ----- .
　　(A) head
　　(B) spirit
　　(C) mind
　　(D) mood

Q9. It has proven to be a ----- success during the past two years.
　　(A) runaway
　　(B) runway
　　(C) ran away
　　(D) ran the way

Q10. A dog is man's best friend, ----- the old saying goes.
　　(A) that
　　(B) when
　　(C) as
　　(D) since

Q11. Older people in these situations often get ----- when they are homebound.
　　(A) depress　　　　　　(B) depressed
　　(C) depressing　　　　(D) to depress

Step 4　解答・解説チェック

現時点での理解度を確認しよう。

問題文は、動物を使った療法を紹介する話です。

1. 正解 **(A)**。質問:「話によると、犬は何をしますか?」。答え:「人の気分をよくする」。ヒント: they can raise people's spirits and get them into a healthier frame of mind.
2. 正解 **(D)**。質問:「『高齢者のための犬』が始まったのは、いつですか?」。答え:「一昨年」。ヒント: and after two years it has proven to be a runaway success.
3. 正解 **(C)**。質問:「話し手は、『高齢者のための犬』についてどう思っていますか?」。答え:「よいこと」。ヒント: 話全体の肯定的な内容から。
4. 正解 **(C)**。質問:「この文書に述べられている療法を受けるのは、誰ですか?」。答え:「高齢者」。ヒント: there's a new kind of therapy ... true for many elderly people
5. 正解 **(A)**。質問:「老人ホームに住む人びとについて、どんなことが言われていますか?」。答え:「うつ状態になる」。ヒント: Older people ... get depressed.
6. 正解 **(D)**。質問:「セラピー・ドッグは、どれくらいの頻度で人びとを訪れますか?」。答え:「月におよそ4〜8回」。ヒント: once or twice a week
7. 正解 **(D)**。選択肢はすべて動詞。文意から、replace「〜に取って代わる」を選ぶ。(A)「〜を再びする」、(B)「〜を改革する」、(C)「〜を作り直す」。
8. 正解 **(C)**。文意から、frame of mind「気分」を完成させる。
9. 正解 **(A)**。文意から、runaway success「大成功」を完成させる。(B)「滑走路」、(C)「逃亡する」。
10. 正解 **(C)**。as を選び、as the old saying goes「古いことわざに言われるように」を完成させる。
11. 正解 **(B)**。depressed（形容詞）を選び、get depressed「うつ状態になる」にする。

Step 5　直読直解トレーニング

速読速聴力を高めよう。
(※日本語訳は、英語の原文の順序どおりに記してあります。)

A dog is man's best friend, as the old saying goes. Now /
犬は人間の最良の友です、ことわざにあるとおり。現在では、
there's a new kind of therapy / which shows / that it's certainly true /
新しいタイプの治療法があります、それが示しています、確かに真実であると、
for many elderly people / who are homebound / or are in nursing homes.
多くの高齢者にとって、外出が困難である、あるいは介護施設に入所している。
Older people / in these situations / often get depressed. Now,
高齢者たちは、こうした状況にある、しばしばうつ状態になります。もちろん、
dogs cannot replace human contact, but they can raise people's spirits /
犬は人間の触れ合いに代わることはできませんが、元気づけることができます、
and get them / into a healthier frame of mind. The "therapy" dogs are /
そして彼らを〜することができます、健全な気持ちに。セラピー・ドッグは、
brought around / to private homes / and nursing homes /
連れて行かれ、個人宅に、そして介護施設に、
once or twice a week / to allow residents / to interact with these animals.
週に1、2回、居住者ができるように、これらの動物との交流を。
This program is called / "Dogs for Seniors," and after two years /
このプログラムは呼ばれています、「高齢者のための犬」と、2年が経過して、
it has proven / to be a runaway success.
わかっています、予想外の大成功であると。

語句

- **saying**：ことわざ
- **elderly**：高齢の
- **situation**：状況
- **replace**：〜に代わる
- **interact**：交流する
- **therapy**：治療
- **homebound**：家から出られない
- **depressed**：うつ状態の
- **resident**：居住者
- **prove**：〜を証明する

Step 6　基本構文トレーニング

文法・語彙力を高めよう。

41	犬は人間の最良の友です。	A dog is man's best friend.
42	新しいタイプの治療法があります。	There's a new kind of therapy.
43	それは、多くの高齢者にとって、確かに真実です。	It's certainly true for many elderly people.
44	こうした状況にある高齢者は、しばしばうつ状態になります。	Older people in these situations often get depressed.
45	犬は、人間同士の触れ合いに代わることはできません。	Dogs cannot replace human contact.
46	犬は、人びとを元気づけることができます。	Dogs can raise people's spirits.
47	犬は、彼らをより健全な気持ちにすることができます。	Dogs can get them into a healthier frame of mind.
48	セラピー・ドッグは、個人宅に連れて行かれます。	The "therapy" dogs are brought around to private homes.
49	このプログラムは、「高齢者のための犬」と呼ばれています。	This program is called "Dogs for Seniors."
50	予想外の大成功であるとわかっています。	It has proven to be a runaway success.

Day 6 チェックテスト

ふさわしい語句の意味を選ぼう。＜制限時間5分＞

1. be backed up：(A) ～を背負って　(B) 渋滞している　(C) ～を基にする
2. exit：(A) 出口　(B) 入口　(C) 引出し
3. involve：(A) 怠惰な　(B) ～を巻き込む　(C) 回転する
4. flatbed：(A) アパート　(B) ゴザ　(C) 平床式の
5. fender-bender：(A) 修理工場　(B) 渋滞　(C) 車同士の接触事故
6. on the scene：(A) 現場に　(B) 目撃して　(C) 撮影で
7. location：(A) 撮影　(B) 場所　(C) 引っ越し
8. clear：(A) 渋滞していない　(B) 迂回する　(C) 順調な
9. the hour：(A) 真夜中　(B) 正午　(C) 正時
10. chopper：(A) ヘリコプター　(B) ナタ　(C) オートバイ

11. highly：(A) 大いに　(B) 礼儀正しい　(C) 高価な
12. fillet：(A) 背びれ　(B) フィレ　(C) 満たすもの
13. big on：(A) 大きすぎる　(B) 重り　(C) ～が大好きで
14. profile：(A) ～を整理する　(B) 書庫　(C) 世間の認知
15. presence：(A) 贈り物　(B) 存在　(C) 現在
16. direct marketing：(A) 卸売り　(B) 直販　(C) 指揮する
17. refill：(A) 給油　(B) ファイルし直す　(C) お代わり
18. afterwards：(A) あとに続く言葉　(B) 戦後　(C) そのあとで
19. contract：(A) 契約書　(B) 請求書　(C) 接触
20. wait on：(A) ～を計る　(B) ～を保留する　(C) ～を重くする

21. adopt：(A) ～を押しつける　(B) ～を確認する　(C) ～を採用する
22. ruling：(A) 判定　(B) 定規　(C) 査定
23. instant：(A) ～の代わりに　(B) 即座の　(C) 変わらない
24. creep in：(A) ねじる　(B) 潜る　(C) 入り込む

25. tradition-bound：(A) 伝統から解放された　(B) 伝統を無視する　(C) 伝統にしばられた
26. implant：(A) 工業化する　(B) 〜をはめ込む　(C) 植林する
27. detect：(A) 〜を検知する　(B) 決める　(C) 技術
28. cross：(A) 〜を横切る　(B) 向こう側　(C) 〜を切る
29. eliminate：(A) 輝く　(B) 〜を反映する　(C) 〜を取り除く
30. disputed：(A) 憤慨した　(B) 争点となっている　(C) 提案された

31. connection：(A) 接触　(B) 連絡　(C) 接続
32. relief：(A) ピッチャー　(B) 木の葉　(C) 安堵
33. slow down：(A) 〜を投げる　(B) 遅れて　(C) 〜を遅くする
34. guess：(A) ゲスト　(B) 推測　(C) 信じる
35. setting：(A) 設定　(B) セットになった　(C) 座ること
36. a bit：(A) 苦味　(B) ほんの少し　(C) 1滴
37. speed up：(A) 〜を話す　(B) 〜のスピードを上げる　(C) 演説
38. walk someone through something：(A) (人)に(物)を手取り足取り教える　(B) 乗り越える　(C) 散歩する
39. solve：(A) 〜を調べる　(B) 〜を解決する　(C) 〜を研究する
40. load：(A) 道路　(B) 荷を下ろす　(C) ロードする

41. saying：(A) 嘘　(B) 迷信　(C) ことわざ
42. therapy：(A) 医院　(B) 健康　(C) 治療
43. elderly：(A) ひじ　(B) 高齢の　(C) より高く
44. homebound：(A) 家に向かって　(B) 家屋が崩壊した　(C) 家から出られない
45. situation：(A) 状況　(B) 座席　(C) 駅
46. depressed：(A) うつ状態の　(B) 印象深い　(C) 潰れた
47. replace：(A) 〜に代わる　(B) 引っ越す　(C) 再生する
48. resident：(A) 社長　(B) 居住者　(C) 大家
49. interact：(A) 交流する　(B) 交差点　(C) 興味深い
50. prove：(A) 〜を弁護する　(B) 証拠　(C) 〜を証明する

チェックテスト解答

1. **(B)**	2. **(A)**	3. **(B)**	4. **(C)**	5. **(C)**
6. **(A)**	7. **(B)**	8. **(A)**	9. **(C)**	10. **(A)**
11. **(A)**	12. **(B)**	13. **(C)**	14. **(C)**	15. **(B)**
16. **(B)**	17. **(C)**	18. **(C)**	19. **(A)**	20. **(B)**
21. **(C)**	22. **(A)**	23. **(B)**	24. **(C)**	25. **(C)**
26. **(B)**	27. **(A)**	28. **(A)**	29. **(C)**	30. **(B)**
31. **(C)**	32. **(C)**	33. **(C)**	34. **(B)**	35. **(A)**
36. **(B)**	37. **(B)**	38. **(A)**	39. **(B)**	40. **(C)**
41. **(C)**	42. **(C)**	43. **(B)**	44. **(C)**	45. **(A)**
46. **(A)**	47. **(A)**	48. **(B)**	49. **(A)**	50. **(C)**

<ワンポイント>

　第1週のトレーニングはいかがでしたか？　やはり、Step 1「リスニング問題」がむずかしく感じられたでしょうか？　繰り返しになりますが、Part 3, 4 の問題形式に慣れることが目的ですから、間違っても気にしないことです。

　問題形式に慣れるという点では、正答できたかどうかより、設問（Q1～Q6）を素早く理解できたことのほうが大事です。Part 3, 4, 7 の設問は、合計108問。設問の意味がすぐにわからなければ、焦って間違うか（Part 3, 4）、解答時間が足りなくなります（Part 7）。

　ですから、Step 4「解答・解説チェック」の際は、設問の意味を正しく理解できていたかを確認することが大事です（選択肢は、正解の意味だけ確認すれば大丈夫です）。

　また、Step 5～6 のトレーニングはいかがでしたか？「トレーニング内容が少し物足りない」「もっとトレーニングしたい」と感じた方には、Week 2（50ページ）、Week 3（86ページ）、Week 4（122ページ）に応用トレーニングを紹介していますので、チャレンジしてみてください。

第3章

Week 2

Week 2
今週のトレーニング

Day 1〜 Day 5のトレーニング			
Step	内容		時間
1	リスニング問題（3問）		2分
2	リーディング問題（3問）		3分
3	文法・語彙問題（5問）		2分
4	解答・解説チェック		3分
5	直読直解トレーニング		5〜15分
	①	CD（英語）を聞いて、英文を目で追う。	
	②	CD（英語）を聞いて、日本語訳を目で追う。	
	③	カンマ (,)、ピリオド (.)、スラッシュ (/) の単位で、英文の意味が理解できるか確認（理解できない部分は、日本語訳や語彙を参照）。	
6	基本構文トレーニング		5〜15分
	①	1文ずつCD（日本語・英語）を聞き、英語を数回音読。	
	②	10文の英語を続けて音読（数回行なう）。	
	③	テキストを縦に半分に折るなどして日本語訳を隠し、英語部分を見て意味がすぐにわかるか確認。	
	④	応用トレーニング「ルックアップ＆セイ」	

＜ワンポイント＞

　先週のトレーニングはいかがでしたか？　少し物足りないと感じた方は、Step 6の④「応用トレーニング」として、以下を追加学習してください。テキストを見ないで基本構文を話す練習で、さらに学習効果が期待できます。

ルックアップ＆セイ	英文を音読したあと、顔を上げて（英文を見ずに）、英文を話す（小声か口パクでもOK）。言えなかった英文は何度か音読し、再チャレンジしてください。

Week 2

Day 1 説明文トレーニング

Step 1 リスニング問題
CDを聞いて、問題を解こう。＜制限時間2分＞

Q1. Who is the announcement aimed at?
 (A) Potential CBSB customers
 (B) Former CBSB employees
 (C) CBSB's new employees
 (D) CBSB executives

Q2. How much must a person keep at CBSB to take advantage of the service?
 (A) $100
 (B) $200
 (C) $500
 (D) $1,000

Q3. What benefit do users of the new service receive?
 (A) They can obtain money from any ATM in the area.
 (B) They get free investment advice.
 (C) They save money.
 (D) They can enjoy free parking.

Step 2　リーディング問題
英文を読んで、問題を解こう。＜制限時間3分＞

Tired of being nickel-and-dimed to death by bank fees? Why not switch to CBSB? As long as you maintain a $1,000 balance in any account or invest $1,000 in CDs, mutual funds, or bonds, we'll waive your bank fees. That's right. You pay nothing for any bill payment, money transfer, withdrawal, and even for buying traveler's checks. With CBSB's Switch Today, we'll even do all the paperwork to make that switch as easy as a walk in the park. So give us a call at 1-800-455-CBSB or drop into any CBSB branch near you and we'll get you started. The world of no-fee banking is yours at CBSB.

Q4.　Where would these words most probably be read?
　　　(A) In a textbook
　　　(B) In a guidebook
　　　(C) In a news report
　　　(D) In an advertisement

Q5.　What is CBSB?
　　　(A) A bank
　　　(B) A mutual fund
　　　(C) A travel agency
　　　(D) A telephone service

Q6.　How can CBSB be contacted for more information?
　　　(A) By fax
　　　(B) By letter
　　　(C) By e-mail
　　　(D) By telephone

Step 3 文法・語彙問題
空欄にふさわしい語句を選ぼう。＜制限時間2分＞

Q7. Tired of being nickel-and-dimed to ----- by bank fees?
 (A) dead
 (B) death
 (C) dying
 (D) be dead

Q8. If you are, why not ----- to CBSB?
 (A) to switch
 (B) switching
 (C) switch
 (D) switched

Q9. If you're interested, drop ----- any CBSB branch near you.
 (A) into
 (B) to
 (C) on
 (D) at

Q10. Come to our branch and we'll get you -----.
 (A) the start
 (B) starting
 (C) start
 (D) started

Q11. The world of no-fee banking is ----- at CBSB.
 (A) you
 (B) your
 (C) yours
 (D) of you

Step 4　解答・解説チェック

現時点での理解度を確認しよう。

問題文は、手数料が無料の銀行取引の広告文です。

1. 正解 **(A)**。質問：「この案内は、誰に向けられたものですか？」。答え：「CBSBの潜在顧客」。ヒント：Tired of being nickel-and-dimed to death by bank fees? Why not switch to CBSB?
2. 正解 **(D)**。質問：「このサービスの特典を受けるには、CBSBにいくら預けておく必要がありますか？」。答え：「1000ドル」。ヒント：As long as you maintain a $1,000 balance..., we'll waive your bank fees.
3. 正解 **(C)**。質問：「新しいサービスの利用客には、どのような利点がありますか？」。答え：「節約」。ヒント：we'll waive your bank fees., You pay nothing
4. 正解 **(D)**。質問：「これらの言葉をもっともよく読むのは、どこだと思われますか？」。答え：「広告」。ヒント：Tired of being nickel-and-dimed to death by bank fees? Why not switch to CBSB?
5. 正解 **(A)**。質問：「CBSBは、何ですか？」。答え：「銀行」。ヒント：The world of no-fee banking is yours at CBSB.
6. 正解 **(D)**。質問：「さらに情報を得るために、どんな方法でCBSBに連絡ができますか？」。答え：「電話で」。ヒント：give us a call at 1-800-455-CBSB
7. 正解 **(B)**。文意から、to death「ひどく（〜する）」を完成させる。
8. 正解 **(C)**。why notに続くのは、動詞の原形。Why not switch 〜? を完成させる。
9. 正解 **(A)**。文意から、drop into「〜に立ち寄る」を完成させる。
10. 正解 **(D)**。文意から、startedを選び、get +（人・物）+ 過去分詞「（人）を〜の状態にする」を完成させる。
11. 正解 **(C)**。文意から、1語で「あなたのもの」を意味する所有格代名詞yoursを選ぶ。

Step 5　直読直解トレーニング
速読速聴力を高めよう。
（※日本語訳は、英語の原文の順序どおりに記してあります。）

Tired of being nickel-and-dimed / to death / by bank fees?
ささいな出費にうんざりしていませんか、心底、銀行手数料の？
Why not switch / to CBSB? As long as you maintain / a $1,000 balance /
切り替えてはいかがですか、CBSBに？　維持する限り、残額1000ドルを、
in any account / or invest $1,000 / in CDs, mutual funds, or bonds,
口座、または1,000ドル投資すれば、CD（譲渡性預金）、投資信託、債券に、
we'll waive your bank fees. That's right. You pay nothing /
銀行手数料を免除します。そうです。無料です、
for any bill payment, money transfer, withdrawal,
どんな料金の支払い、送金、引き出し、
or even for buying traveler's checks. With CBSB's Switch Today,
さらには、トラベラーズチェックの購入も。CBSBのスイッチ・トゥデイでは、
we'll even do all the paperwork / to make that switch /
書類手続きさえもすべて私どもがいたします、そうした切り替えをするために、
as easy as a walk in the park. So / give us a call / at 1-800-455-CBSB /
いとも簡単に。ですから、お電話ください、1-800-455-CBSBに、
or drop into / any CBSB branch near you / and we'll get you started.
またはお立ち寄りください、お近くのCBSB支店に、開始の準備をいたします。
The world of no-fee banking is yours / at CBSB.
無料バンキングの世界があなたのものに、CBSBで。

語句			
maintain：〜を維持する		balance：残高	
account：口座		invest：〜を投資する	
waive：〜を免除する		bill：請求書	
payment：支払い		money transfer：送金	
withdrawal：引き出し		branch：支店	

Step 6　基本構文トレーニング

文法・語彙力を高めよう。

51	ささいな出費に心底うんざりしていませんか？	Tired of being nickel-and-dimed to death?
52	CBSB に切り替えてはいかがですか？	Why not switch to CBSB?
53	あなたの銀行手数料を免除します。	We'll waive your bank fees.
54	どんな料金の支払いも、すべて無料です。	You pay nothing for any bill payment.
55	書類手続きさえも、すべて私どもがいたします。	We'll even do all the paperwork.
56	それは、いとも簡単です。	It's as easy as a walk in the park.
57	1-800-455-CBSB にお電話ください。	Give us a call at 1-800-455-CBSB.
58	お近くの CBSB 支店にお立ち寄りください。	Drop into any CBSB branch near you.
59	私どもが、開始の準備をいたします。	We'll get you started.
60	CBSB で、無料バンキングの世界があなたのものに。	The world of no-fee banking is yours at CBSB.

Day 2 会話文トレーニング

Step 1 リスニング問題
CDを聞いて、問題を解こう。＜制限時間2分＞

Q1. Where are the speakers?
　　(A) In their office
　　(B) In their home
　　(C) In their car
　　(D) In their backyard

Q2. Probably who are the speakers?
　　(A) A husband and wife
　　(B) A brother and sister
　　(C) A mother and son
　　(D) A grandfather and granddaughter

Q3. What did the woman just do?
　　(A) Take Sandy to the neighbors' house
　　(B) Get up
　　(C) Clean out the refrigerator
　　(D) Enter the house

Step 2　リーディング問題

英文を読んで、問題を解こう。＜制限時間3分＞

W:　Hey, Oliver, I'm home. Sandy, are you upstairs? Come on down. Mommy's home.
M:　She's out. I took her over to the Turners for her play date.

W:　Uh, Oliver, look at the calendar here on the refrigerator. What do you see?
M:　Yeah, it says "Play date, 3:30 p.m. with Janice."
W:　And what day is today?

W:　It's OK. I called Mrs. Turner. She says Janice was home anyway and the two girls are having fun playing video games.
M:　Thank goodness for that. Sorry about that, honey. I really thought today was Tuesday.

Q4.　Who is Sandy?
　　　(A) The man's wife　　　　　(B) The man's mother
　　　(C) The couple's friend　　　(D) The couple's daughter

Q5.　Where is Sandy?
　　　(A) At home　　　　　　　　(B) Upstairs
　　　(C) At the Turners' house　　(D) In a video game center

Q6. What was the man mistaken about?
　　　(A) What day it was
　　　(B) What time it was
　　　(C) The address of Mrs. Turner
　　　(D) The name of Sandy's friend

Step 3　文法・語彙問題
空欄にふさわしい語句を選ぼう。＜制限時間2分＞

Q7. Thank goodness ---- that, because I was worried about them.
   (A) to
   (B) with
   (C) from
   (D) for

Q8. ---- about that; I promise to be more careful next time.
   (A) Bad
   (B) Regret
   (C) Sorry
   (D) Ashamed

Q9. I ---- today was Tuesday, but actually it's Wednesday.
   (A) think
   (B) thought
   (C) knew
   (D) know

Q10. Look at the calendar here on the refrigerator and tell me what it ----.
   (A) shows
   (B) says
   (C) tells
   (D) looks

Q11. They are having fun ---- video games and doing other things.
   (A) played
   (B) to play
   (C) playing
   (D) having played

Step 4　解答・解説チェック

現時点での理解度を確認しよう。

問題文は、曜日を間違えて子供を隣人宅に連れて行ってしまったカップルの会話です。

1. 正解 **(B)**。質問:「話し手たちは、どこにいますか？」。答え:「彼らの家」。ヒント：I'm home.
2. 正解 **(A)**。質問:「話し手たちは、どんな人だと思われますか？」。答え:「夫婦」。ヒント：Mommy's home., Sorry about that, honey.
3. 正解 **(D)**。質問:「女性は、何をしたところですか？」。答え:「家に入った」。ヒント：I'm home.
4. 正解 **(D)**。質問:「サンディは、どんな人物ですか？」。答え:「カップルの娘」。ヒント：Mommy's home.
5. 正解 **(C)**。質問:「サンディは、どこにいますか？」。答え:「ターナー家」。ヒント：I took her over to the Turners
6. 正解 **(A)**。質問:「男性が間違えたのは、何ですか？」。答え:「その日の曜日」。ヒント：I really thought today was Tuesday.
7. 正解 **(D)**。文意から、thank goodness for that「それはよかった」を完成させる。
8. 正解 **(C)**。文意から、Sorry about that.「それはすみませんでした」を完成させる。that は、「相手が指摘した内容」を指している。
9. 正解 **(B)**。was が過去形なので、時制の一致で、thought（過去形）を選ぶ。(C) も過去形だが、「知っていました」で、文意に合わない。
10. 正解 **(B)**。選択肢は、すべて動詞の3人称単数現在形。文意から、says「〜と書いてある」を選ぶ。
11. 正解 **(C)**。playing（現在分詞）を選び、have fun + 動詞 ing「〜をして楽しむ」の現在進行形を完成させる。

Step 5　直読直解トレーニング
速読速聴力を高めよう。
（※日本語訳は、英語の原文の順序どおりに記してあります。）

W:　Hey, Oliver, I'm home. Sandy, are you upstairs?
　　ねえ、オリバー、ただいま。サンディ、2階にいるの？
　　Come on down. Mommy's home.
　　降りてきて。お母さんが帰ってきたわ。
M:　She's out. I took her over / to the Turners / for her play date.
　　出かけてるよ。連れて行った、ターナーさんの家へ、遊びの約束で。

W:　Uh, Oliver, look at the calendar / here on the refrigerator.
　　あのね、オリバー、カレンダーを見てよ、冷蔵庫のここの。
　　What do you see?
　　何が見える？
M:　Yeah, it says / "Play date, 3:30 p.m. with Janice."
　　ええ、書いてあるね、「遊びの約束、午後3時30分にジャニスと」と。
W:　And what day is today?
　　それで、今日は何曜日なの？

W:　It's OK. I called Mrs. Turner. She says / Janice was home /
　　大丈夫。ターナー夫人に電話したよ。言ってるよ、ジャニスは家にいて、
　　anyway / and the two girls are having fun / playing video games.
　　いずれにしても、2人で楽しんでいる、テレビゲームをして。
M:　Thank goodness for that. Sorry about that, honey.
　　それはよかった。ごめんなさい。
　　I really thought / today was Tuesday.
　　本当に思ったよ、今日は火曜日だと。

語句　be home：帰宅して　upstairs：上の階に　come on down：降りてくる
out：出かけている　play date：遊びの約束　refrigerator：冷蔵庫　say：〜と書いてある
have fun：楽しむ　video game：テレビゲーム　Thank goodness：ありがたい！

Step 6　基本構文トレーニング

文法・語彙力を高めよう。

61	ただいま。	I'm home.
62	私が彼女をターナーさんの家へ連れて行きました。	I took her over to the Turners.
63	冷蔵庫のここのカレンダーを見てください。	Look at the calendar here on the refrigerator.
64	何が見えますか？	What do you see?
65	「ジャニスと午後3時30分に遊びの約束」と書いてあります。	It says "Play date, 3:30 p.m. with Janice."
66	今日は何曜日ですか？	What day is today?
67	彼女らは、楽しくテレビゲームをして遊んでいます。	They are having fun playing video games.
68	それは、よかったです。	Thank goodness for that.
69	それは、すみませんでした。	Sorry about that.
70	今日は火曜日だと思っていました。	I thought today was Tuesday.

Week 2

Day 3　説明文トレーニング

Step 1　リスニング問題
CD を聞いて、問題を解こう。＜制限時間 2 分＞

Q1. What is the speaker worried about?
　　(A) The training of pilots
　　(B) Safety at airports
　　(C) Overbooked flights
　　(D) Expensive airline tickets

Q2. How will most listeners probably react to the announcement?
　　(A) They will become worried.
　　(B) They will be pleased.
　　(C) They will become excited.
　　(D) They will be confused.

Q3. If authorities pay attention to the announcement, what will they do?
　　(A) Send more undercover reporters to major airports
　　(B) Hire more experienced pilots
　　(C) Reduce the number of security personnel
　　(D) Try to make airports safer

Step 2　リーディング問題

英文を読んで、問題を解こう。＜制限時間3分＞

As everyone knows, airport security seems to have been tightened up. There are more police; screening procedures are stronger; security staff are better trained. However, the reality is something quite different, according to the Bragg Group for International Awareness and Cooperation. In a confidential report, they claim that airports are not more secure than they were before 9/11. They say that much of the beefing up of security is superficial. They sent undercover reporters into 25 major airports across the globe, where they found numerous flaws in the new security measures. The full details are available online on the group's Web site, but in summary, a lot more work needs to be done to make our airports completely safe.

Q4.　How do the writers of the report feel about airport security?
(A) Angry　　　　　　　　(B) Confident
(C) Doubtful　　　　　　　(D) Pleased

Q5.　What is said about increased security since 9/11?
(A) It is no better than it was before 9/11.
(B) The government is covering up the truth.
(C) It is actually worse than it was before 9/11.
(D) Much of it only appears to be better.

Q6.　Can more information be obtained from the Bragg Group?
(A) Yes, on the Internet.
(B) Yes, by writing to them.
(C) No. The information is confidential.
(D) No. The government controls the information.

Step 3　文法・語彙問題
空欄にふさわしい語句を選ぼう。＜制限時間２分＞

Q7. As everyone knows, airport security seems to have been ----- up.
   (A) tighten
   (B) tightened
   (C) to tighten
   (D) being tight

Q8. Compared to the past, security staff are ----- trained now.
   (A) better to be
   (B) better be
   (C) better
   (D) to better

Q9. They say much of the beefing ----- of security is superficial.
   (A) up
   (B) down
   (C) out
   (D) on

Q10. The reality is ----- quite different from what it should be.
   (A) somewhat
   (B) something like
   (C) something
   (D) some kind of

Q11. They sent ----- reporters into 25 major airports to check the new security measures.
   (A) under the cover
   (B) under a cover
   (C) covered-up
   (D) undercover

Step 4　解答・解説チェック

現時点での理解度を確認しよう。

問題文は、空港のセキュリティの現状について述べたものです。

1. 正解 **(B)**。質問：「話し手の懸念は、何ですか？」。答え：「空港の安全」。ヒント：話の内容全体から。
2. 正解 **(A)**。質問：「この案内を、聞き手はどのように受け取ると思われますか？」。答え：「不安になる」。ヒント：they claim that airports are not more secure than they were before 9/11., They say that much of the beefing up of security is superficial., … a lot more work needs to be done to make our airports completely safe. などから。
3. 正解 **(D)**。質問：「当局がこの案内に注目した場合、何をしますか？」。答え：「空港をより安全にしようとする」。ヒント：Q2 同様。
4. 正解 **(C)**。質問：「書き手は、空港のセキュリティについてどう感じていますか？」。答え：「疑わしい」。ヒント：a lot more work needs to be done to make our airports completely safe.
5. 正解 **(D)**。質問：「9・11 以降のセキュリティの強化についてどんなことが述べられていますか？」。答え：「ほとんどは、よくなっているように見えるにすぎない」。ヒント：much of the beefing up of security is superficial.
6. 正解 **(A)**。質問：「ブラッグ・グループからより多くの情報を得ることは可能ですか？」。答え：「はい、インターネット上で」。ヒント：The full details are available online on the group's Web site,
7. 正解 **(B)**。have been のあとなので tightened を選び、tighten up「厳しくする」の受動態を完成させる。
8. 正解 **(C)**。文意から、better trained「よりよく訓練されている」にする。
9. 正解 **(A)**。文意から、beef up「強化する」の動名詞を完成させる。
10. 正解 **(C)**。something (quite) different「（まったく）異なる何か」にする。(A) は、quite がなければ、somewhat different「いくぶん異なる」で可。
11. 正解 **(D)**。文意から、undercover reporters「覆面レポーター」を完成させる。

Step 5　直読直解トレーニング
速読速聴力を高めよう。
(※日本語訳は、英語の原文の順序どおりに記してあります。)

As everyone knows, airport security seems / to have been tightened up.
みなさんご存じのように、空港の安全チェックは〜ようです、厳しくなった。
There are more police; screening procedures are stronger;
警官は増強され、審査手続きは強化され、
security staff are better trained. However, the reality /
警備員はより訓練されています。しかし、現実は、
is something quite different, according to the Bragg Group /
まったく違います、ブラッグ・グループによると
for International Awareness and Cooperation. In a confidential report,
国際意識と協力のための。極秘報告書で、
they claim / that airports are not more secure / than they were before 9/11.
彼らは訴えています、空港は安全になってはいないと、9.11以前よりも。
They say / that much of the beefing up of security / is superficial.
彼らは述べています、安全強化の大部分は、表面上だけだと。
They sent undercover reporters / into 25 major airports across the globe,
彼らは、覆面レポーターを派遣しました、世界の25の主要空港に、
where they found numerous flaws / in the new security measures.
そこで彼らは多くの欠陥を見つけました、新しい安全対策に。
The full details are available online / on the group's Web site,
詳細はネットで入手できます、同グループのウェブサイトから、
but in summary, a lot more work needs to be done /
しかし要約すると、もっとたくさんすべきことがあります、
to make our airports completely safe.
われわれの空港を完全に安全にするために。

語句
screening：審査　procedure：手続き　confidential：機密の　claim：〜を訴える
secure：安全な　superficial：表面的な　numerous：多数の　flaw：欠陥
measure：対策　available：利用できる

Step 6　基本構文トレーニング
文法・語彙力を高めよう。

71	空港の安全チェックは厳しくなったようです。	Airport security seems to have been tightened up.
72	審査手続きが、さらに強化されています。	Screening procedures are stronger.
73	警備員は、より訓練されています。	Security staff are better trained.
74	現実は、まったく違います。	The reality is something quite different.
75	彼らは、空港はより安全になってはいないと訴えています。	They claim that airports are not more secure.
76	安全強化の大部分は表面上だけです。	Much of the beefing up of security is superficial.
77	彼らは、25の主要空港に覆面レポーターを派遣しました。	They sent undercover reporters into 25 major airports.
78	彼らは、新しい安全対策に多くの欠陥を見つけました。	They found numerous flaws in the new security measures.
79	詳細は、ネットで入手できます。	The full details are available online.
80	もっとたくさんすべきことがあります。	A lot more work needs to be done.

Day 4　会話文トレーニング

Step 1　リスニング問題
CD を聞いて、問題を解こう。＜制限時間 2 分＞

Q1. Where are the people planning to go?
　　(A) To a hotel
　　(B) To a restaurant
　　(C) To Italy
　　(D) To Chicago

Q2. What the people talking about?
　　(A) When the man's parents got married
　　(B) What to order at Olivia's
　　(C) Who will attend the gathering
　　(D) How much they will spend at Olivia's

Q3. Who is uncertain about attending the gathering?
　　(A) The woman
　　(B) The man
　　(C) The man's parents
　　(D) Aunt Jessica and Uncle Bert

Step 2　リーディング問題
英文を読んで、問題を解こう。＜制限時間３分＞

W: So, where are you taking your parents on their anniversary?
M: The plan is to take them to Olivia's. That's the Italian bistro we've been talking about. It's the one in Berrisdale.

W: Will Uncle Verne be coming?
M: No, he's out of town at some conference in Chicago.
W: So I guess it'll just be us, Bob and his wife—and Aunt Jessica and Uncle Bert.

W: Wait a minute, Ron. I think I have to work on the 17th, because that might be when Penelope's starting her vacation.
M: Really? Can't you get someone else to cover for you that day?

Q4. Who is having an anniversary?
　　(A) Jessica and Bert
　　(B) An interview
　　(C) Bob and his wife
　　(D) Ron's parents

Q5. How many people will be at the anniversary dinner?
　　(A) Three or four　　　(B) Four or five
　　(C) Five or six　　　　(D) Six or seven

Q6. Who definitely will NOT be at Olivia's on the 17th?
　　(A) Bob and Olivia
　　(B) Uncle Verne
　　(C) Aunt Jessica and Uncle Bert
　　(D) The man and the woman who are speaking

Step 3　文法・語彙問題
空欄にふさわしい語句を選ぼう。＜制限時間2分＞

Q7. He's out ---- town at some conference in Chicago, so he can't come.
（A）for
（B）off
（C）from
（D）of

Q8. The 17th? That might be ---- Penelope's starting her vacation.
（A）date
（B）time
（C）when
（D）where

Q9. Can't you get someone ---- to cover for you at the office?
（A）change
（B）another
（C）person
（D）else

Q10. The plan is ----- them to Olivia's on their anniversary.
（A）take
（B）to take
（C）about taking
（D）for taking

Q11. That's the Italian bistro we've been ----- about.
（A）saying
（B）speaking
（C）telling
（D）talking

Step 4　解答・解説チェック

現時点での理解度を確認しよう。

問題文は、両親の結婚記念日を計画する男女の会話です。

1. 正解 **(B)**。質問：「話し手たちは、どこへ行く予定ですか？」。答え：「レストラン」。ヒント：The plan is to take them to Olivia's. That's the Italian bistro
2. 正解 **(C)**。質問：「話し手たちは、何について話していますか？」。答え：「誰が集まりに出席するか」。ヒント：Will Uncle Verne be coming?, No, he's out of town at some conference in Chicago., So I guess it'll just be us, Bob and his wife—and Aunt Jessica and Uncle Bert.
3. 正解 **(A)**。質問：「集まりに出席することが決まっていない人は、誰ですか？」。答え：「女性」。ヒント：I think I have to work on the 17th
4. 正解 **(D)**。質問：「記念日を迎えるのは、誰ですか？」。答え：「ロンの両親」。ヒント：where are you taking your parents...?
5. 正解 **(C)**。質問：「記念日の夕食に出席するのは、何人ですか？」。答え：「5人か6人」。ヒント：So I guess it'll just be us, Bob and his wife—and Aunt Jessica and Uncle Bert., I think I have to work on the 17th
6. 正解 **(B)**。質問：「17日に確実にオリビアにいないのは、誰ですか？」。答え：「バーン伯父」。ヒント：Will Uncle Verne be coming?, No, he's out of town
7. 正解 **(D)**。文意から、out of town「遠出をしている」を完成させる。
8. 正解 **(C)**。2つの節を結んで意味をなす when を選ぶ。
9. 正解 **(D)**。文意から、someone else「誰か他の人」を完成させる。at the office は、「職場で」。
10. 正解 **(B)**。be 動詞（is）のあとなので、名詞（相当語句）を選ぶ。to take「連れて行くこと」を選ぶ。taking（動名詞）でも可。
11. 正解 **(D)**。talk about「〜について話す」を完成させる。tell は、tell +（人）+ about で、「（人）に〜について話す」。

Step 5　直読直解トレーニング

速読速聴力を高めよう。

（※日本語訳は、英語の原文の順序どおりに記してあります。）

W: So, where are you taking your parents / on their anniversary?
　　それで、あなたの両親をどこへ連れて行くのですか、結婚記念日に？

M: The plan is / to take them / to Olivia's. That's the Italian bistro /
　　計画は、連れて行くものです、オリビアに。イタリアン・ビストロです、
　　we've been talking about. It's the one in Berrisdale.
　　われわれが話していた。それは、ベリスデールにあるものです。

W: Will Uncle Verne be coming?
　　バーン伯父さんは来ますか？

M: No, he's out of town / at some conference / in Chicago.
　　いえ、彼は出張中です、何かの会議に、シカゴでの。

W: So / I guess / it'll just be / us, Bob and his wife—
　　だとすると、思います、だけになると、われわれと、ボブと彼の奥さん、
　　and Aunt Jessica and Uncle Bert.
　　それにジェシカ伯母さんとバート伯父さん。

W: Wait a minute, Ron. I think / I have to work / on the 17th,
　　ちょっと待って、ロン。思います、働かなければならないと、17日は、
　　because / that might be / when Penelope's starting her vacation.
　　なぜなら、それはたぶん、ペネロピーが休暇に入る日なので。

M: Really? Can't you get someone else / to cover for you / that day?
　　本当？　誰かほかの人にしてもらえないのですか、代わりを、その日に？

語句

anniversary：記念日［ここでは結婚記念日］　bistro：ビストロ［イタリアの居酒屋］
uncle：おじ　　　　　　　　　　　　　　out of town：遠出をしている
conference：会議　　　　　　　　　　　　aunt：おば
wait a minute：ちょっと待って　　　　　 vacation：休暇
someone else：ほかの誰か　　　　　　　　cover：代わりをする

Step 6　基本構文トレーニング
文法・語彙力を高めよう。

81	結婚記念日にあなたの両親をどこへ連れて行きますか？	Where are you taking your parents on their anniversary?
82	計画は、彼らをオリビアへ連れて行くというものです。	The plan is to take them to Olivia's.
83	それは、われわれが話していたイタリアン・ビストロです。	That's the Italian bistro we've been talking about.
84	それは、ベリスデールにあるものです。	It's the one in Berrisdale.
85	バーン伯父さんは来ますか？	Will Uncle Verne be coming?
86	彼はシカゴでの何かの会議で出張中です。	He's out of town at some conference in Chicago.
87	われわれだけだと思います。	I guess it'll just be us.
88	17日は、働かなければならないと思います。	I think I have to work on the 17th.
89	それは、たぶんペネロピーが休暇に入る日です。	That might be when Penelope's starting her vacation.
90	誰かほかの人に代わってもらえないのですか？	Can't you get someone else to cover for you?

Day 5 説明文トレーニング

Step 1 リスニング問題
CDを聞いて、問題を解こう。＜制限時間2分＞

Q1. What is "Mystery Island"?
　　(A) A novel
　　(B) A theme park
　　(C) A television program
　　(D) A song

Q2. What is the purpose of the talk?
　　(A) To explain how "Mystery Island" got started
　　(B) To talk about the future of "Mystery Island"
　　(C) To announce the end of "Mystery Island"
　　(D) To describe what is wrong with "Mystery Island"

Q3. Who are Chris Nielsen and Sasha Cabral?
　　(A) Actors
　　(B) Mystery writers
　　(C) Regular viewers of "Mystery Island"
　　(D) Producers of an upcoming mini-series

Step 2　リーディング問題

英文を読んで、問題を解こう。＜制限時間３分＞

"Mystery Island" had a sensational first season last year. When the season ended, a lot of loose ends hadn't been tied up, so there's plenty for viewers to look forward to in the next season. The producer, Annabella Benetti, has dropped some hints about the first half of the season, which will be like a mini-series. She says there will be fairly straightforward storylines. What's on the other side of the island? That will be revealed in due time, but it's probably not what most fans think it is. Also, there will be two new members of the cast, Chris Nielsen and Sasha Cabral. Nielsen is a veteran TV actor, but for Cabral, from Brazil, it will be her first English-speaking role.

Q4. How many seasons of the show have been on the air so far?
 (A) One
 (B) One and a half
 (C) Two
 (D) Two and a half

Q5. What mystery does the writer refer to?
 (A) How the next season ends
 (B) Who the new actors are
 (C) What is on the other side of the island
 (D) When the first season will end

Q6. What is true of Chris Nielsen and Sasha Cabral?
 (A) They are from Brazil.
 (B) They did not appear in the first season.
 (C) They and Annabella Benetti are actors.
 (D) They helped to produce the program.

Step 3　文法・語彙問題

空欄にふさわしい語句を選ぼう。＜制限時間2分＞

Q7. According to the newspaper, "Mystery Island" had ----- first season last year.
　　(A) a sensation
　　(B) a sensational
　　(C) sensations
　　(D) sensationally

Q8. There's plenty ----- viewers to look forward to in the next season.
　　(A) which
　　(B) that
　　(C) for
　　(D) to

Q9. Nobody knows the answer to "What's on ----- side of the island?"
　　(A) another
　　(B) other
　　(C) others
　　(D) the other

Q10. It's probably not what ----- fans think it is.
　　(A) most of
　　(B) almost
　　(C) most
　　(D) the most

Q11. It will be her first ----- role in her 15-year career as an actress.
　　(A) speaking-English
　　(B) English-speaking
　　(C) English-spoken
　　(D) spoken-English

Step 4　解答・解説チェック

現時点での理解度を確認しよう。

問題文は、2年目のシーズンを迎えるテレビドラマの紹介です。

1. 正解 **(C)**。質問：「ミステリー・アイランドとは、何ですか？」。答え：「テレビ番組」。ヒント：When the season ended, a lot of loose ends hadn't been tied up
2. 正解 **(B)**。質問：「この話の目的は、何ですか？」。答え：「ミステリー・アイランドの先行きについて話す」。ヒント：The producer, Annabella Benetti, has dropped some hints about the first half of the season,
3. 正解 **(A)**。質問：「クリス・ニールセンとサーシャ・キャブラルは、どんな人ですか？」。答え：「俳優」。ヒント：there will be two new members of the cast, Chris Nielsen and Sasha Cabral.
4. 正解 **(A)**。質問：「この番組は、これまでに何シーズン分放映されましたか？」。答え：「1シーズン」。ヒント："Mystery Island" had a sensational first season last year.
5. 正解 **(C)**。質問：「書き手は、どんなミステリーに言及していますか？」。答え：「島の反対側に何があるか」。ヒント：She says there will be fairly straightforward storylines. What's on the other side of the island?
6. 正解 **(B)**。質問：「クリス・ニールセンとサーシャ・キャブラルに関して、正しい記述はどれですか？」。答え：「彼らは初シーズンに登場していない」。ヒント：there will be two new members of the cast
7. 正解 **(B)**。文意から、a sensational first season「センセーショナルな初シーズン」を完成させる。
8. 正解 **(C)**。文意から、for +（人・物）+ to + 動詞「（人・物）にとって〜するための」を完成させる。
9. 正解 **(D)**。文意から、on the other side「反対側に」を完成させる。
10. 正解 **(C)**。文意から、most fans「ほとんどのファン」を完成させる。（A）は、most of the なら可。
11. 正解 **(B)**。名詞 role「役」の前なので、形容詞、English-speaking「英語を話す」を選ぶ。

Step 5　直読直解トレーニング
速読速聴力を高めよう。
(※日本語訳は、英語の原文の順序どおりに記してあります。)

"Mystery Island" had / a sensational first season /
「ミステリー・アイランド」は迎えました、センセーショナルな初シーズンを、
last year. When the season ended, a lot of loose ends /
昨年。シーズンが終わった時点で、たくさんの未解決の問題が、
hadn't been tied up, so there's plenty for viewers / to look forward to /
解決されていませんでした、ですから視聴者にはたくさんあります、楽しみが、
in the next season. The producer, Annabella Benetti,
次期シーズンに。プロデューサーの、アンナベッラ・ベネッティは、
has dropped some hints / about the first half of the season,
多少のヒントを与えています、シーズンの前半について、
which will be like a mini-series. She says / there will be /
それはミニシリーズのようです。彼女は語っています、それらはなるだろうと、
fairly straightforward storylines. What's on the other side of the island?
かなりわかりやすい筋書に。島の反対側に何があるのでしょうか？
That will be revealed / in due time, but it's probably not /
それは明らかにされるでしょう、いずれ、しかしそれはたぶん違うでしょう、
what most fans think it is. Also, there will be /
ほとんどのファンが考えているものとは。また、登場します、
two new members of the cast, Chris Nielsen and Sasha Cabral.
2人の新しい出演者が、クリス・ニールセンとサーシャ・キャブラルです。
Nielsen is a veteran TV actor, but for Cabral,
ニールセンはベテランのテレビ俳優です、しかしキャブラルにとっては、
from Brazil, it will be her first English-speaking role.
ブラジル出身の、それは彼女の初めての英語を話す役になります。

語句	
loose end：未解決の問題　**tie up**：〜を完了させる　**viewer**：視聴者	
look forward to：〜を楽しみに待つ　**straightforward**：わかりやすい　**storyline**：筋書	
in due time：いずれ　**cast**：出演者　**veteran**：経験豊かな　**role**：役	

Step 6　基本構文トレーニング
文法・語彙力を高めよう。

91	「ミステリー・アイランド」は、センセーショナルな初シーズンを迎えました。	"Mystery Island" had a sensational first season.
92	たくさんの未解決な問題が解決していませんでした。	A lot of loose ends hadn't been tied up.
93	視聴者には、楽しみがたくさんあります。	There's plenty for viewers to look forward to.
94	プロデューサーは、多少ヒントを与えています。	The producer has dropped some hints.
95	島の反対側に、何があるのでしょうか？	What's on the other side of the island?
96	それは、いずれ明らかにされるでしょう。	That will be revealed in due time.
97	それは、たぶん多くのファンが考えているのとは違うものでしょう。	It's probably not what most fans think it is.
98	2人の新しい出演者が登場します。	There will be two new members of the cast.
99	ニールセンはベテランのテレビ俳優です。	Nielsen is a veteran TV actor.
100	それは、彼女の初めての英語を話す役になります。	It will be her first English-speaking role.

Day 6 チェックテスト

ふさわしい語句の意味を選ぼう。＜制限時間5分＞

1. maintain：(A) ～を交換する　(B) ～を移植する　(C) ～を維持する
2. balance：(A) 入金　(B) 出金　(C) 残高
3. account：(A) 交換　(B) ～を計算する　(C) 口座
4. invest：(A) ～を投資する　(B) ～を探検する　(C) ～を発明する
5. waive：(A) 波　(B) 風変わりな　(C) ～を免除する
6. bill：(A) 請求書　(B) 建物　(C) 領収書
7. payment：(A) 請求　(B) 支払い　(C) 罰金
8. money transfer：(A) 両替　(B) 送金　(C) 為替
9. withdrawal：(A) 引き出し　(B) 預け入れ　(C) 記帳
10. branch：(A) 支店　(B) 本店　(C) 部署

11. be home：(A) 帰省して　(B) 家の中　(C) 帰宅して
12. upstairs：(A) 階段を上る　(B) 上の階に　(C) 階段の上部
13. come on down：(A) 倒れる　(B) 立ち上がる　(C) 降りてくる
14. out：(A) 出かけている　(B) 外出する　(C) 失敗する
15. play date：(A) 観劇　(B) 遊ぶ日　(C) 遊びの約束
16. refrigerator：(A) 冷蔵庫　(B) 交渉人　(C) 反抗
17. say：(A) たとえば　(B) ～を歌う　(C) ～と書いてある
18. have fun：(A) うちわを持っている　(B) 人気のある　(C) 楽しむ
19. video game：(A) 試合を録画する　(B) テレビゲーム　(C) 試合の収録
20. Thank goodness：(A) いやはや　(B) ありがとう　(C) ありがたい

21. screening：(A) 映画館　(B) 叫ぶ　(C) 審査
22. procedure：(A) 完了　(B) 進行　(C) 手続き
23. confidential：(A) 機密の　(B) 自信に満ちた　(C) 重要な
24. claim：(A) 文句を言う　(B) ～を訴える　(C) 手荷物
25. secure：(A) 安全な　(B) 危険な　(C) 完全な

26. superficial：(A) 物理的な　(B) 表面的な　(C) 超人的な
27. numerous：(A) 満場一致の　(B) 多数の　(C) 匿名の
28. flaw：(A) 飛ぶ　(B) 流れ　(C) 欠陥
29. measure：(A) 対策　(B) 専攻　(C) 原因
30. available：(A) 利用できる　(B) 収益　(C) 可能性

31. anniversary：(A) 記念日　(B) 大学　(C) 式典
32. bistro：(A) 調理器具　(B) 食器　(C) ビストロ
33. uncle：(A) かかと　(B) 甥　(C) おじ
34. out of town：(A) 田舎にいる　(B) 遠出をしている　(C) 町を出て行く
35. conference：(A) 確信　(B) 会議　(C) 練習
36. aunt：(A) おば　(B) おばあさん　(C) 姪
37. wait a minute：(A) ちょっと待って　(B) 急いで　(C) ごゆっくり
38. vacation：(A) 欠員　(B) 清掃　(C) 休暇
39. someone else：(A) 代わりの誰か　(B) 誰でも　(C) 他の誰か
40. cover：(A) お代わりを頼む　(B) 交換する　(C) 代わりをする

41. loose end：(A) 最後に負ける　(B) 緩んだ結び目　(C) 未解決の問題
42. tie up：(A) 〜をつかむ　(B) 〜を発射する　(C) 〜を完了させる
43. viewer：(A) 視聴者　(B) 監督　(C) 顕微鏡
44. look forward to：(A) 〜を楽しみに待つ　(B) 前を見る　(C) 〜を探す
45. straightforward：(A) 前向きな　(B) わかりやすい　(C) 直線道路
46. storyline：(A) 筋書　(B) 河口　(C) 蒸気船
47. in due time：(A) 予定時刻に　(B) いずれ　(C) 締め切りまでに
48. cast：(A) 出演者　(B) 予報　(C) くじ
49. veteran：(A) ベトナム人の　(B) 年老いた　(C) 経験豊かな
50. role：(A) 規則　(B) 巻物　(C) 役

チェックテスト解答

1. **(C)**	2. **(C)**	3. **(C)**	4. **(A)**	5. **(C)**
6. **(A)**	7. **(B)**	8. **(B)**	9. **(A)**	10. **(A)**
11. **(C)**	12. **(B)**	13. **(C)**	14. **(A)**	15. **(C)**
16. **(A)**	17. **(C)**	18. **(C)**	19. **(B)**	20. **(C)**
21. **(C)**	22. **(C)**	23. **(A)**	24. **(B)**	25. **(A)**
26. **(B)**	27. **(B)**	28. **(C)**	29. **(A)**	30. **(A)**
31. **(A)**	32. **(C)**	33. **(C)**	34. **(B)**	35. **(B)**
36. **(A)**	37. **(A)**	38. **(C)**	39. **(C)**	40. **(C)**
41. **(C)**	42. **(C)**	43. **(A)**	44. **(A)**	45. **(B)**
46. **(A)**	47. **(B)**	48. **(A)**	49. **(C)**	50. **(C)**

<ワンポイント>

　第2週のトレーニングはいかがでしたか？　設問（Q1～Q6）を素早く理解できるようになってきましたか？　設問が素早く理解できるようになってきたら、問題形式に慣れてきたと考えていいと思います。

　しかし、問題形式には慣れてきたけれど、「英語がさっぱり聞き取れない」という方も多いはずです。リスニング上達のコツは、いきなり母国語のように100％聞き取れることを期待しないこと。70％聞き取れたら十分ぐらいの気持ちで「リラックスして聞く」ことです。

　わからないところがあっても、気にしない。わからないところに意識を向けるのではなく、わかったところから想像する。いい力の加減で聞きましょう。リスニング力は、想像力。会話やスピーチの場面（WhoとWhere）を想像しながら聞き、問題を解きながら、わからなかったところも想像してみましょう。

第**4**章

Week 3

Week 3
今週のトレーニング

Day 1〜 Day 5 のトレーニング			
Step	内容		時間
1	リスニング問題（3問）		2分
2	リーディング問題（3問）		3分
3	文法・語彙問題（5問）		2分
4	解答・解説チェック		3分
5	直読直解トレーニング		5〜15分
	①	CD（英語）を聞いて、英文を目で追う。	
	②	CD（英語）を聞いて、日本語訳を目で追う。	
	③	カンマ（,）、ピリオド（.）、スラッシュ（/）の単位で、英文の意味が理解できるか確認（理解できない部分は、日本語訳や語彙を参照）。	
6	基本構文トレーニング		5〜15分
	①	1文ずつCD（日本語・英語）を聞き、英語を数回音読。	
	②	10文の英語を続けて音読（数回行なう）。	
	③	テキストを縦に半分に折るなどして日本語訳を隠し、英語部分を見て意味がすぐにわかるか確認。	
	④	応用トレーニング「ルックアップ＆セイ」「音読筆写」	

＜ワンポイント＞

　先週の応用トレーニング「ルックアップ＆セイ」（50ページ）を、試してみましたか？　どうしても顔を上げて言えない基本構文は、音読筆写をしてみると、しっかり覚えることができます。

音読筆写	英文を声に出しながら、スピードを上げて5回書き写します（字は乱れてOK）。終了したら、顔を上げ、英語を話します（言えなかったら、あと2回音読筆写）。

Day 1　説明文トレーニング

Step 1　リスニング問題
CDを聞いて、問題を解こう。＜制限時間2分＞

Q1. Which of the following does the speaker mention?
 (A) A famous jazz singer
 (B) A famous jazz event
 (C) A famous jazz song
 (D) A famous jazz group

Q2. What is making more people listen to jazz?
 (A) Movies
 (B) Television
 (C) Satellite radio
 (D) CDs and DVDs

Q3. What is true of jazz today?
 (A) It is very popular.
 (B) It is popular only with older people.
 (C) It is rarely heard on the radio.
 (D) It is seldom performed live.

Step 2 リーディング問題
英文を読んで、問題を解こう。＜制限時間３分＞

Maybe it seems jazz was the music your parents' or your grandparents' generation listened to. It may come as a surprise, then, to know that jazz is thriving in the 21st century. The biggest jazz festival in the world, the Monterey (California) Jazz Festival, set an attendance record last year. All five major concert acts sold out their shows completely, so how could jazz be dead? Anyone who thinks so is sadly mistaken. Jazz aficionados can tell you there are many more talented artists playing jazz today than even ten years ago. Also the satellite radio boom has helped, because it has exposed jazz to a wider audience than traditional AM or FM radio does.

Q4. What surprise does the writer mention?
 (A) That readers' grandparents listened to jazz
 (B) That jazz is very popular today
 (C) That jazz is slowly dying with the older generation
 (D) That Monterey has a jazz festival

Q5. What does the writer say about the death of jazz?
 (A) It is not true.
 (B) It cannot be helped.
 (C) It is very sad.
 (D) It has already happened.

Q6. What has increased in the past ten years?
 (A) The number of AM and FM radio stations
 (B) The number of performing jazz artists
 (C) The number of jazz festivals
 (D) The number of concert acts at Monterey

Step 3　文法・語彙問題
空欄にふさわしい語句を選ぼう。＜制限時間２分＞

Q7. Maybe it seems jazz was the music your ----- generation listened to.
   (A) parent
   (B) parent's
   (C) parents'
   (D) parents

Q8. The biggest jazz festival set an ----- record last year.
   (A) attend
   (B) attending
   (C) attendance
   (D) attended

Q9. Believe it or not, all five ----- sold out their shows completely.
   (A) concerts act
   (B) concert actions
   (C) concert act
   (D) concert acts

Q10. There are many more talented artists ----- jazz today than even ten years ago.
   (A) play
   (B) playing
   (C) are playing
   (D) played

Q11. It has ----- jazz to a wider audience all over the world.
   (A) been exposed
   (B) exposed
   (C) expressed
   (D) expected

Step 4　解答・解説チェック

現時点での理解度を確認しよう。

問題文は、ジャズに、流行の兆しがあることを伝える内容です。

1. 正解 **(B)**。質問：「話し手が述べているのは、次のどれですか？」。答え：「有名なジャズイベント」。ヒント：The biggest jazz festival in the world
2. 正解 **(C)**。質問：「より多くの人にジャズを聞かせるものは、何ですか？」。答え：「衛星ラジオ」。ヒント：Also the satellite radio boom has helped
3. 正解 **(A)**。質問：「今日のジャズについて、正しい記述はどれですか？」。答え：「とても人気がある」。ヒント：to know that jazz is thriving
4. 正解 **(B)**。質問：「書き手は、どんな意外なことを述べていますか？」。答え：「ジャズが今日大人気である」。ヒント：It may come as a surprise, then, to know that jazz is thriving in the 21st century.
5. 正解 **(A)**。質問：「書き手は、ジャズの衰退について何と言っていますか？」。答え：「事実ではない」。ヒント：Anyone who thinks so is sadly mistaken.
6. 正解 **(B)**。質問：「過去10年間で増えたことは、何ですか？」。答え：「ジャズ演奏家の数」。ヒント：there are many more talented artists playing jazz today than even ten years ago.
7. 正解 **(C)**。名詞 generation の前なので、名詞の所有格がくる。「両親の」という文意から、parents'（複数名詞の所有格）を選ぶ。
8. 正解 **(C)**。文意から、set an attendance record「入場者数の新記録を打ち立てる」を完成させる。
9. 正解 **(D)**。five のあとなので、名詞の複数形がくる。concert acts「コンサート（という出し物）」（複数形）を選ぶ。
10. 正解 **(B)**。artists をうしろから修飾する現在分詞 playing を選び、artists playing jazz「ジャズを演奏するアーティスト」を完成させる。
11. 正解 **(B)**。選択肢は、すべて動詞の変化形。has があるので、exposed を選び、expose +（人・物）+ to「（人・物）を〜に広める」の現在完了形を完成させる。

Step 5　直読直解トレーニング

速読速聴力を高めよう。
（※日本語訳は、英語の原文の順序どおりに記してあります。）

Maybe it seems / jazz was the music / your parents' /
思われるかもしれません、ジャズは音楽だったと、あなたの両親、
or your grandparents' generation listened to. It may come as a surprise,
あるいは祖父母の世代が聞いていた。驚かれるかもしれません、
then, to know / that jazz is thriving / in the 21st century.
ですから、知ると、ジャズが繁栄していると、21世紀に。
The biggest jazz festival in the world, the Monterey (California)
世界最大のジャズフェスティバル、モントレー（カリフォルニア）
Jazz Festival, set an attendance record / last year.
ジャズフェスティバルは、入場者数の新記録を打ち立てました、昨年。
All five major concert acts sold out / their shows completely, so /
5大コンサートとも完売でした、チケットはすべて、ですから、
how could jazz be dead? Anyone who thinks so / is sadly mistaken.
ジャズは廃れていません。そう考えている人は、大きな思い違いをしています。
Jazz aficionados can tell you / there are many more talented artists /
ジャズの熱狂的ファンは言うでしょう、もっと有能なアーティストがいると、
playing jazz today / than even ten years ago. Also /
今日ジャズを演奏している、わずか10年前よりも。また、
the satellite radio boom has helped, because it has exposed jazz /
衛星ラジオブームが拍車をかけています、ジャズを広めたからです、
to a wider audience / than traditional AM or FM radio does.
より広い層の聴衆に、従来のAMやFMラジオ放送よりも。

語句			
grandparent：祖父母		generation：世代	
thrive：繁栄する		sell out：〜を売りつくす	
dead：廃れた		sadly：不幸にも	
mistaken：間違った		aficionado：ファン	
satellite：衛星の		expose：〜を広める	

Step 6　基本構文トレーニング
文法・語彙力を高めよう。

101	ジャズはあなたの両親の世代が聞いた音楽です。	Jazz was the music your parents' generation listened to.
102	それに、驚かれるかもしれません。	It may come as a surprise.
103	21世紀にジャズが繁栄しています。	Jazz is thriving in the 21st century.
104	世界最大のジャズフェスティバルが入場者数の新記録を打ち立てました。	The biggest jazz festival set an attendance record.
105	5大コンサートとも、チケットはすべて完売でした。	All five concert acts sold out their shows completely.
106	ジャズは廃れてなどいません。	How could jazz be dead?
107	そう考えている人は、大きな思い違いをしています。	Anyone who thinks so is sadly mistaken.
108	今日、多くのもっと才能あるアーティストがジャズを演奏しています。	There are many more talented artists playing jazz today.
109	衛星ラジオのブームが拍車をかけています。	The satellite radio boom has helped.
110	それは、より広い層の聴衆にジャズを広めました。	It has exposed jazz to a wider audience.

Day 2　会話文トレーニング

Step 1　リスニング問題
CDを聞いて、問題を解こう。＜制限時間2分＞

Q1. What is the man doing?
　　(A) Watching TV
　　(B) Playing a sport
　　(C) Looking at a newspaper
　　(D) Studying a map of Australia

Q2. Where are the people thinking of going?
　　(A) To Australia
　　(B) To a movie
　　(C) To a baseball game
　　(D) To bed

Q3. What did the man and the woman forget?
　　(A) The name of an actor
　　(B) The time of a show
　　(C) The title of a movie
　　(D) The location of a theater

Step 2　リーディング問題

英文を読んで、問題を解こう。＜制限時間3分＞

W: Pass me the movie listings, will you, honey?
M: Let me see if I can find them. Sports...Business...here we are: Entertainment.

W: Are you interested in seeing *Alien Invasion*? It got a good review.
M: Yeah, but that guy I hate is in it. You know, the Australian actor. What's his name?
W: Oh, yeah, I know who you mean, but his name escapes me.

W: So *Count on Me* is on at 4:20, 6:10, 8:00, and 9:50.
M: Can we make the 4:20? What time is it now?

Q4. When does this conversation probably take place?
　　(A) In the morning　　　　(B) In the afternoon
　　(C) In the early evening　　(D) In the late evening

Q5. How long is *Count on Me*?
　　(A) About 1 hour
　　(B) 1 hour and 20 minutes
　　(C) A little less than 2 hours
　　(D) A little more than 2 hours

Q6. How does the man feel about *Alien Invasion*?
　　(A) He does not want to see it.
　　(B) He heard that it was not good.
　　(C) He thinks it might be interesting.
　　(D) He thinks it was made in Australia.

Step 3 文法・語彙問題
空欄にふさわしい語句を選ぼう。＜制限時間2分＞

Q7. Are you ---- in seeing *Alien Invasion* or some other movie?
 (A) interesting
 (B) interested
 (C) interest
 (D) interests

Q8. That guy I hate is ---- it, so I don't want to see that movie.
 (A) on
 (B) to
 (C) of
 (D) in

Q9. I know ---- you mean, but I can't remember his name.
 (A) who
 (B) why
 (C) how
 (D) where

Q10. Let me ---- if I can find them somewhere here on the sofa.
 (A) to see
 (B) seeing
 (C) see
 (D) be seen

Q11. It's already 2:00. Can we ---- the 4:20?
 (A) meet
 (B) make
 (C) have
 (D) go

Step 4　解答・解説チェック

現時点での理解度を確認しよう。

問題文は、映画を観に行こうと考えている夫婦の会話です。

1. 正解 **(C)**。質問:「男性は、何をしていますか?」。答え:「新聞を見ている」。ヒント: Pass me the movie listings, will you, honey?, Let me see if I can find them.
2. 正解 **(B)**。質問:「話し手たちは、どこに行こうと思っていますか?」。答え:「映画」。ヒント: Can we make the 4:20?
3. 正解 **(A)**。質問:「この男女は、何を忘れましたか?」。答え:「俳優の名前」。ヒント: I know who you mean, but his name escapes me.
4. 正解 **(B)**。質問:「この会話が行なわれているのは、いつだと思われますか?」。答え:「午後」。ヒント: Can we make the 4:20?
5. 正解 **(C)**。質問:「『カウント・オン・ミー』の上映時間は、どれくらいですか?」。答え:「2時間弱」。ヒント: *Count on Me* is on at 4:20, 6:10, 8:00, and 9:50.
6. 正解 **(A)**。質問:「男性は、『エイリアンの侵略』をどう感じていますか?」。答え:「観たくない」。ヒント: that guy I hate is in it.
7. 正解 **(B)**。文意から、be interested in + 動詞 ing「〜することに興味がある」の疑問文を完成させる。
8. 正解 **(D)**。文意から、「〜に出演している」を表わす前置詞 in を選ぶ。
9. 正解 **(A)**。文意から、who you mean「あなたが誰のことを言っているのか」という名詞節を完成させる。
10. 正解 **(C)**。文意から、let me + 動詞で、「(自分が)〜する」を完成させる。
11. 正解 **(B)**。文意から、「間に合う」を意味する make を選ぶ。

Step 5　直読直解トレーニング

速読速聴力を高めよう。

(※日本語訳は、英語の原文の順序どおりに記してあります。)

W: Pass me the movie listings, will you, honey?
　　映画欄を取ってくれますか、あなた？
M: Let me see if / I can find them.
　　ええと、見つけられるでしょうか。
　　Sports...Business...here we are: Entertainment.
　　スポーツ、ビジネス、あった、エンテーテイメントだ。

W: Are you interested / in seeing *Alien Invasion*?
　　興味がありますか、『エイリアンの侵略』を観ることに？
　　It got a good review.
　　評判はいいです。
M: Yeah, but that guy I hate is in it. You know, the Australian actor.
　　ああ、でも大嫌いな男が出ています。ほら、オーストラリア人の俳優の。
　　What's his name?
　　彼は、何という名前でしたっけ？
W: Oh, yeah, I know who you mean, but his name escapes me.
　　ええ、はい、誰のことかわかります、でも彼の名前を思い出せません。

W: So / *Count on Me* is on /
　　それで、『カウント・オン・ミー』は上映されます、
　　at 4:20, 6:10, 8:00, and 9:50.
　　4時20分、6時10分、8時、それと9時50分に。
M: Can we make the 4:20? What time is it now?
　　4時20分の回に間に合いますか？　今何時ですか？

語句
pass：〜を手渡す　**listings**：番組表　**let me see**：ええと　**here we are**：あった
entertainment：娯楽　**alien**：異星人　**invasion**：侵略　**review**：批評
you know：ほら　**escape**：逃げる

Step 6　基本構文トレーニング
文法・語彙力を高めよう。

111	映画欄を取ってくれますか？	Pass me the movie listings, will you?
112	ええと、見つけられるでしょうか。	Let me see if I can find them.
113	『エイリアンの侵略』を観ることに興味がありますか？	Are you interested in seeing *Alien Invasion*?
114	評判はいいです。	It got a good review.
115	私の大嫌いな男が出ています。	That guy I hate is in it.
116	彼は、何という名前でしたっけ？	What's his name?
117	誰のことを言っているかわかります。	I know who you mean.
118	彼の名前を思い出せません。	His name escapes me.
119	『カウント・オン・ミー』は、4時20分に上映されます。	*Count on Me* is on at 4:20.
120	4時20分の回に、間に合いますか？	Can we make the 4:20?

Day 3　説明文トレーニング

Step 1　リスニング問題

CDを聞いて、問題を解こう。＜制限時間2分＞

Q1. What is the talk about?

(A) Pets

(B) Wild animals

(C) Animals in zoos

(D) Farm animals

Q2. Why were some animals captured?

(A) They were needed for zoos.

(B) They were sick.

(C) They were dangerous.

(D) They were needed for experiments.

Q3. What is causing problems like leopard attacks in Mumbai?

(A) Bigger cities

(B) Global warming

(C) Smaller budgets

(D) Food shortages

Step 2　リーディング問題
英文を読んで、問題を解こう。＜制限時間3分＞

As urban sprawl increases in India, a new threat has emerged. Many cities are now infringing on the wildlife of the jungle and plains. It's not just monkeys wandering into towns to steal food. Elephants and leopards have caused destruction of property and attacked humans. For example, the city government of Mumbai grew so concerned over leopard attacks that it had to do something. It organized its animal welfare forces and rounded up 47 of these wandering leopards. They were then released back into a national park, where officials can only hope they will stay.

Q4.　What is causing the problem that is described in the passage?
　(A) Cities are growing larger.
　(B) More animals are being born.
　(C) People do not have enough food.
　(D) Wild animals are moving into the plains.

Q5.　How many different kinds of wild animals are named?
　(A) Two
　(B) Three
　(C) Four
　(D) Five

Q6.　What is NOT mentioned about wild animals?
　(A) They have destroyed property.
　(B) They have attacked humans.
　(C) They have killed people.
　(D) They have been caught and moved.

Step 3　文法・語彙問題
空欄にふさわしい語句を選ぼう。＜制限時間2分＞

Q7. As urban sprawl increases, a new ----- has emerged from the forest.
　　(A) threat
　　(B) throw
　　(C) welfare
　　(D) stock

Q8. Many cities are now infringing ----- the wildlife of the jungle.
　　(A) on
　　(B) at
　　(C) to
　　(D) over

Q9. They have caused destruction of property and ----- humans.
　　(A) attacks
　　(B) attacked
　　(C) attacking
　　(D) have been attacked

Q10. It rounded ----- 47 of these wandering leopards.
　　(A) out
　　(B) about
　　(C) up
　　(D) down

Q11. Officials can only ----- they will stay outside the city.
　　(A) wish
　　(B) hope
　　(C) release
　　(D) concern

Step 4　解答・解説チェック
現時点での理解度を確認しよう。

問題文は、都市の乱開発が招いた野生動物の問題についての話です。

1. 正解 **(B)**。質問:「この話は、何についてですか?」。答え:「野生動物」。ヒント: Many cities are now infringing on the wildlife of the jungle and plains.
2. 正解 **(C)**。質問:「動物たちが捕獲されたのは、なぜですか?」。答え:「危険だったから」。ヒント: Elephants and leopards have caused destruction of property and attacked humans.
3. 正解 **(A)**。質問:「ムンバイでのヒョウの攻撃のような問題が起こる原因は、何ですか?」。答え:「都市部の拡大」。ヒント: As urban sprawl increases in India, a new threat has emerged.
4. 正解 **(A)**。質問:「この文面で取り上げている問題の原因になっているのは、何ですか?」。答え:「都市がますます大きくなっている」。ヒント: As urban sprawl increases in India, a new threat has emerged.
5. 正解 **(B)**。質問:「何種類の野生動物の名前が述べられていますか?」。答え:「3種類」。ヒント: monkeys, Elephants and leopards
6. 正解 **(C)**。質問:「野生動物について、述べられていないことは何ですか?」。答え:「人間たちを殺した」。ヒント: (A) have caused destruction of property, (B) and attacked humans, (D) rounded up 47 of these wandering leopards. They were then released back into a national park
7. 正解 **(A)**。文意から、threat「脅威」を選ぶ。
8. 正解 **(A)**。文意から、infringe on「～(の権利)を侵害する」の現在進行形を完成させる。
9. 正解 **(B)**。選択肢はすべて動詞 attack の語形。主語は They で、and で結ばれた2つの動詞の語形は同形になるので、attacked を選ぶ。
10. 正解 **(C)**。文意から、round up「～を一斉に捕獲する」の過去形を完成させる。
11. 正解 **(B)**。hope を選び、can only hope「(できることは)～を望むだけ」を完成させる。will があるので、(A) wish は不可。

Step 5　直読直解トレーニング

速読速聴力を高めよう。

（※日本語訳は、英語の原文の順序どおりに記してあります。）

As urban sprawl increases / in India, a new threat has emerged.
都市化が進む中、インドで、新たな脅威が生まれました。
Many cities are / now infringing / on the wildlife / of the jungle and plains.
多くの都市が、いまや権利を侵害しています、野生生物の、ジャングルや草原の。
It's not just monkeys / wandering into towns / to steal food.
それはサルだけではありません、街に迷い込んでくる、食料を盗むために。
Elephants and leopards / have caused destruction / of property /
ゾウやヒョウは、破壊しています、財産を、
and attacked humans. For example, the city government of Mumbai /
そして人間を襲っています。たとえば、ムンバイの市当局は、
grew so concerned / over leopard attacks / that it had to do something.
非常に懸念し、ヒョウの攻撃を、何らかの手を打たなくてはなりませんでした。
It organized / its animal welfare forces / and rounded up /
そこは組織し、動物愛護団を、そして一斉に捕獲しました、
47 of these wandering leopards. They were then / released back /
出没するヒョウ47頭を。それらはその後、放されました、
into a national park, where officials / can only hope / they will stay.
国立公園に、そこで係員たちは、期待するだけです、彼らが留まることを。

語句			
urban sprawl：都市開発		**emerge**：出現する	
wildlife：野生生物		**plains**：草原	
wander：さまよう		**destruction**：破壊	
property：財産		**concerned**：懸念して	
organize：〜を組織する		**release**：〜を解放する	

Step 6　基本構文トレーニング
文法・語彙力を高めよう。

121	新たな脅威が生まれました。	A new threat has emerged.
122	今や多くの都市が野生生物の権利を侵害しています。	Many cities are now infringing on the wildlife.
123	それは、街に迷い込んでくるサルだけではありません。	It's not just monkeys wandering into towns.
124	彼らは、財産を破壊し、そして人間を襲っています。	They have caused destruction of property and attacked humans.
125	市当局はヒョウの攻撃を、懸念し始めました。	The city government grew concerned over leopard attacks.
126	そこは、何らかの手を打たなくてはなりませんでした。	It had to do something.
127	そこは、動物愛護団を組織しました。	It organized its animal welfare forces.
128	それは、出没するヒョウ47頭を一斉に捕獲しました。	It rounded up 47 of these wandering leopards.
129	それらは、その後、国立公園に放されました。	They were then released back into a national park.
130	係員たちは、彼らが留まってくれることを期待するだけです。	Officials can only hope they will stay.

Day 4　会話文トレーニング

Step 1　リスニング問題
CD を聞いて、問題を解こう。＜制限時間 2 分＞

Q1. Where did the conversation take place?
　　(A) On an airplane
　　(B) On a train
　　(C) In an elevator
　　(D) In a high-rise building

Q2. What is the man going to do soon?
　　(A) Move to Addison
　　(B) Meet his wife's family for the first time
　　(C) Speak to some people
　　(D) Have a job interview at an architecture firm

Q3. How long have the two people known each other?
　　(A) For a very short time
　　(B) For years
　　(C) Since they were young
　　(D) Since they studied architecture together

Step 2　リーディング問題

英文を読んで、問題を解こう。＜制限時間3分＞

M: Excuse me. Is Finch the next stop?
W: No, it's much farther up the line. I'm getting off at Finch, so don't worry.

M: Actually, I'm making a presentation today and I'm a little nervous. This is the first time I've even met these people.
W: You'll be fine. What exactly do you do, if you don't mind my asking?
M: I don't mind at all. I'm an architect with a firm based in Addison.

M: It was nice talking to you. Thanks for getting me pointed in the right direction.
W: No problem whatsoever. Good luck with your presentation.

Q4. How many stations or cities are mentioned?
　　(A) One　　　　　　　　(B) Two
　　(C) Three　　　　　　　(D) Four

Q5. Why does the woman tell the man not to worry?
　　(A) Because he is doing a good job
　　(B) Because Finch is not the next stop
　　(C) Because he can get off the train when she does
　　(D) Because she thinks his presentation will be fine

Q6. What does the woman ask the man about?
　　(A) His work
　　(B) Where he lives
　　(C) His presentation
　　(D) Where he is going

Step 3　文法・語彙問題
空欄にふさわしい語句を選ぼう。＜制限時間2分＞

Q7. It's much farther ----- the line, about an hour from here.
   (A) to
   (B) with
   (C) up
   (D) upon

Q8. I'm ----- a presentation today to a large group of people.
   (A) telling
   (B) making
   (C) speaking
   (D) putting

Q9. I'm ----- little nervous because I've never done it before.
   (A) a
   (B) some
   (C) the
   (D) that

Q10. I'm an architect with a firm ----- in Addison.
   (A) basing
   (B) it's based
   (C) is basing
   (D) based

Q11. Thanks for getting me pointed in the ----- direction.
   (A) good
   (B) left
   (C) smooth
   (D) right

Step 4　解答・解説チェック

現時点での理解度を確認しよう。

問題文は、自分の降りる駅がわからない男性と女性の会話です。

1. 正解 **(B)**。質問：「この会話は、どこで行なわれましたか？」。答え：「電車の中」。ヒント：it's much farther up the line.
2. 正解 **(C)**。質問：「男性は、間もなく何をしますか？」。答え：「何人かの人を相手に話す」。ヒント：I'm making a presentation today
3. 正解 **(A)**。質問：「2人が知り合ってから、どのくらい経っていますか？」。答え：「ほんのわずかの期間」。ヒント：最初のやり取りから。
4. 正解 **(B)**。質問：「いくつの駅名や都市名が述べられていますか？」。答え：「2つ」。ヒント：Finch, Addison
5. 正解 **(C)**。質問：「女性は、なぜ男性に心配することはないと言っているのですか？」。答え：「女性が降りる時に一緒に電車を降りればよいから」。ヒント：I'm getting off at Finch, so don't worry.
6. 正解 **(A)**。質問：「女性は、男性に何を尋ねましたか？」。答え：「彼の仕事」。ヒント：What exactly do you do, if you don't mind my asking?
7. 正解 **(C)**。文意から、up the line「この沿線上の」を完成させる。
8. 正解 **(B)**。文意から、make a presentation「プレゼンを行なう」の現在進行形を完成させる。
9. 正解 **(A)**。文意から、a little「少し」を完成させる。
10. 正解 **(D)**。文意から、based in + 地名「〜を本拠地とする」を完成させる。
11. 正解 **(D)**。文意から、get +（人）+ pointed in the right direction「（人）に正しい方向を示す」を完成させる。

Step 5　直読直解トレーニング

速読速聴力を高めよう。
(※日本語訳は、英語の原文の順序どおりに記してあります。)

M: Excuse me. Is Finch the next stop?
　　すみません。フィンチは次の駅ですか？
W: No, it's much farther up the line. I'm getting off at Finch,
　　いえ、もっとずっと先です。私はフィンチで降ります、
　　so don't worry.
　　ですからご心配なく。

M: Actually, I'm making a presentation / today / and I'm a little nervous.
　　実は、プレゼンをするのです、今日、それで少し不安です。
　　This is the first time / I've even met these people.
　　これが初めてです、その人たちに会うことさえ。
W: You'll be fine. What exactly do you do, if you don't mind my asking?
　　大丈夫ですよ。正確にはお仕事は何ですか、お聞きしてもよかったら？
M: I don't mind at all. I'm an architect / with a firm based / in Addison.
　　まったくかまいません。建築家です、会社に勤める、アディソンにある。

M: It was nice talking to you.
　　あなたとお話しできてよかったです。
　　Thanks for / getting me pointed in the right direction.
　　ありがとうございました、道案内してくださって。
W: No problem whatsoever. Good luck / with your presentation.
　　どういたしまして。がんばってください、プレゼンを。

語句

get off：下車する	**presentation**：プレゼン
nervous：不安な	**exactly**：正確には
at all：[否定文で] まったく	**architect**：建築家
firm：会社	**based in**：〜を本拠地とする
direction：道案内	**whatsoever**：少しも

Step 6　基本構文トレーニング
文法・語彙力を高めよう。

131	フィンチは、次の駅ですか？	Is Finch the next stop?
132	それは、もっとずっと先です。	It's much farther up the line.
133	今日、プレゼンをすることになっています。	I'm making a presentation today.
134	少し不安です。	I'm a little nervous.
135	その人たちに会うことさえ、これが初めてです。	This is the first time I've even met these people.
136	正確には、お仕事は何ですか？	What exactly do you do?
137	まったくかまいません。	I don't mind at all.
138	アディソンにある会社に勤める建築家です。	I'm an architect with a firm based in Addison.
139	あなたと、お話しできてよかったです。	It was nice talking to you.
140	道案内してくださって、ありがとうございました。	Thanks for getting me pointed in the right direction.

Day 5　説明文トレーニング

Step 1　リスニング問題
CD を聞いて、問題を解こう。＜制限時間 2 分＞

Q1. At whom is the talk aimed?
　　(A) People thinking about finding a different job
　　(B) People who have retired from work
　　(C) People about to take their first job
　　(D) People who love their careers

Q2. Which of the following best describes the talk?
　　(A) Advice on making a lot of money quickly
　　(B) Suggestions for those who might change jobs
　　(C) Recommendations for working with difficult colleagues
　　(D) Hints for those about to have job interviews

Q3. Before making a career change, what should people do?
　　(A) Save a large amount of money
　　(B) Discuss the plan with friends and family
　　(C) Think about the best way to do it
　　(D) Attend job-counseling workshops

Step 2 リーディング問題
英文を読んで、問題を解こう。＜制限時間3分＞

Many people think about changing careers, but they are afraid to take the first step. Making a career change does hold some risks. Even so, there is no rule saying you must quit your current job to do so. You can change careers in steps. Night school allows you to balance work and study to learn new job skills. Some people moonlight at a new job in their free time to get a foot in the door. Or some are able to go part-time at their old job and start working part-time at their new career without any overall loss of income. Changing careers just requires a little creative thought.

Q4. According to the passage, why do some people not change careers?
　　(A) Because it is too dangerous
　　(B) Because it involves some risks
　　(C) Because they are too old to change
　　(D) Because they do not want to leave their friends

Q5. What is recommended?
　　(A) Making a change gradually, in steps
　　(B) Talking first to one's friends and family
　　(C) Getting advice from an employment agency
　　(D) Quitting one's current job before searching for a new one

Q6. What are going to night school, moonlighting, and working part-time examples of?
　　(A) Risks that cannot be avoided
　　(B) Opportunities for meeting interesting people
　　(C) Ways to avoid a decision about a job change
　　(D) Possible steps in the process of changing careers

Step 3　文法・語彙問題

空欄にふさわしい語句を選ぼう。＜制限時間2分＞

Q7.　They are afraid to ----- the first step, although they want to change.
　　（A）walk
　　（B）take
　　（C）move
　　（D）put

Q8.　You can change careers ----- steps, not all at once.
　　（A）in
　　（B）on
　　（C）for
　　（D）at

Q9.　Night school ----- you to balance work and study.
　　（A）makes
　　（B）shows
　　（C）learns
　　（D）allows

Q10.　Some people ----- at a new job to get a foot in the door.
　　（A）moonlight
　　（B）sunlight
　　（C）light
　　（D）flashlight

Q11.　Changing careers just requires a little ----- thought.
　　（A）create
　　（B）creative
　　（C）created
　　（D）creation

Step 4　解答・解説チェック

現時点での理解度を確認しよう。

問題文は、転職についてのアドバイスを伝える内容です。

1. 正解 **(A)**。質問：「この話は、誰に向けられたものですか？」。答え：「別な仕事を探そうとしている人」。ヒント：You can change careers in steps.
2. 正解 **(B)**。質問：「この話をもっともよく表わしているのは、次のどれですか？」。答え：「転職するかもしれない人に対する提案」。ヒント：話の内容全体から。
3. 正解 **(C)**。質問：「転職する前にすべきことは、何ですか？」。答え：「最善の方法を考えること」。ヒント：there is no rule saying you must quit your current job to do so. You can change careers in steps.
4. 正解 **(B)**。質問：「この文書によると、なぜ転職をしない人がいるのですか？」。答え：「リスクを伴うから」。ヒント：Making a career change does hold some risks.
5. 正解 **(A)**。質問：「何が推奨されていますか？」。答え：「少しずつ、手順を踏んで転職すること」。ヒント：You can change careers in steps.
6. 正解 **(D)**。質問：「夜間スクール、夜間のアルバイト、パートの仕事は、何の例ですか？」。答え：「転職への足固め」。ヒント：Night school allows..., Some people moonlight, Or some are able to go part-time
7. 正解 **(B)**。文意から、take the first step「一歩を踏み出す」を完成させる。
8. 正解 **(A)**。文意から、in steps「段階を踏んで」を完成させる。
9. 正解 **(D)**。allows を選び、（物・事）+ allow +（人）+ to + 動詞「（物・事）が、（人）が〜することを可能にする」の3人称単数現在形を完成させる。
10. 正解 **(A)**。文意から、moonlight「（副業として）夜間にアルバイトをする」を選ぶ。
11. 正解 **(B)**。名詞 thought「思考」の前なので、形容詞 creative「創造的な」を選ぶ。(A)「〜を創造する」(動詞)、(C)「〜を創造した」(過去形)、(D)「創造」(名詞)。

Step 5　直読直解トレーニング
速読速聴力を高めよう。

(※日本語訳は、英語の原文の順序どおりに記してあります。)

Many people think about / changing careers, but they are afraid /
多くの人が考えます、転職を、しかし彼らは恐れてできません、
to take the first step. Making a career change / does hold some risks.
一歩を踏み出すことが。転職には、確かにリスクが伴います。
Even so, there is no rule / saying you must quit your current job / to do so.
しかし、決まりはありません、今の仕事を辞めなければならない、そのために。
You can change careers in steps. Night school allows you / to balance /
段階を踏んで職を変えることができます。夜間学校が可能にします、両立を、
work and study / to learn new job skills. Some people moonlight /
仕事と学習の、新しい職業技能を習得する。夜間アルバイトをする人もいます、
at a new job / in their free time / to get a foot in the door. Or /
新しい仕事で、彼らの自由時間に、きっかけをつかむために。また、
some are able / to go part-time / at their old job / and start /
できる人もいます、パートタイムを、以前の仕事で、そして始めることを、
working part-time / at their new career / without any overall loss /
パートタイムで働き、新しい仕事で、全体として減らすことなく、
of income. Changing careers just requires / a little creative thought.
収入を。転職には必要なだけです、多少の創造的思考が。

語句

- **career**：職業
- **even so**：たとえそうだとしても
- **quit**：〜を辞める
- **moonlight**：夜間のアルバイトをする
- **income**：収入
- **risk**：リスク
- **saying**：〜という
- **current**：現在の
- **overall**：すべてを含めた
- **creative**：創造的な

Step 6 基本構文トレーニング

文法・語彙力を高めよう。

141	多くの人が転職を考えます。	Many people think about changing careers.
142	彼らは、恐れて一歩を踏み出すことができません。	They are afraid to take the first step.
143	転職には、確かにリスクが伴います。	Making a career change does hold some risks.
144	そうするために、今の仕事を辞めなければなりません。	You must quit your current job to do so.
145	段階を踏んで、職を変えることができます。	You can change careers in steps.
146	夜間学校が、仕事と学習の両立を可能にします。	Night school allows you to balance work and study.
147	それが、新しい職業技術を習得するための学習を可能にします。	It allows you to study to learn new job skills.
148	新しい仕事で、夜間のアルバイトをする人もいます。	Some people moonlight at a new job.
149	以前の仕事で、パートタイムできる人もいます。	Some are able to go part-time at their old job.
150	転職には、多少の創造的思考が必要なだけです。	Changing careers just requires a little creative thought.

Day 6 チェックテスト

ふさわしい語句の意味を選ぼう。＜制限時間5分＞

1. grandparent：(A) 祖父母　(B) 孫　(C) 偉大な両親
2. generation：(A) 世間一般　(B) 加速　(C) 世代
3. thrive：(A) 建築する　(B) 荒廃する　(C) 繁栄する
4. sell out：(A) 〜を売りつくす　(B) 売れ残る　(C) 出航する
5. dead：(A) 眠った　(B) 廃れた　(C) ぶつかった
6. sadly：(A) 突然に　(B) 不幸にも　(C) 偶然にも
7. mistaken：(A) 間違った　(B) 誤配の　(C) 騙された
8. aficionado：(A) 楽曲　(B) デザート　(C) ファン
9. satellite：(A) 衛星　(B) スタジオ　(C) 薄明かり
10. expose：(A) 〜を広める　(B) 言い訳する　(C) 〜のポーズを取る

11. pass：(A) 〜を否決する　(B) 〜を受け取る　(C) 〜を手渡す
12. listings：(A) 電話帳　(B) 番組表　(C) ダイレクトメール
13. let me see：(A) ええと　(B) ですから　(C) まとめますと
14. here we are：(A) どうぞ　(B) あった　(C) こっちです
15. entertainment：(A) 食事　(B) 娯楽　(C) 観光
16. alien：(A) 新人　(B) 原住民　(C) 異星人
17. invasion：(A) 破壊　(B) 開発　(C) 侵略
18. review：(A) 批評　(B) 〜を反転させる　(C) 議論する
19. you know：(A) ほら　(B) ぜひとも　(C) だから
20. escape：(A) 岬　(B) 逃げる　(C) 登る

21. urban sprawl：(A) 郊外　(B) 都市開発　(C) 商店街
22. emerge：(A) 消える　(B) 緊急の　(C) 出現する
23. wildlife：(A) 野生生物　(B) 野獣　(C) 自然体験
24. plains：(A) 無地の　(B) 湿地　(C) 草原
25. wander：(A) 追い込む　(B) さまよう　(C) 忍び込む

26. destruction：(A) 消化　(B) 阻害　(C) 破壊
27. property：(A) 独自の　(B) 貧困　(C) 財産
28. concerned：(A) 懸念して　(B) 安心して　(C) 一緒に
29. organize：(A) 〜を聴く　(B) 〜を組織する　(C) 〜に教える
30. release：(A) 〜を貸し出す　(B) 〜に首輪をする　(C) 〜を解放する

31. get off：(A) 下車する　(B) 乗車する　(C) 飛び込む
32. presentation：(A) 抑圧　(B) 出席　(C) プレゼン
33. nervous：(A) 安心した　(B) くつろいだ　(C) 不安な
34. exactly：(A) 正確には　(B) 現実には　(C) 意外にも
35. at all：(A) とても　(B) まったく　(C) すべてに
36. architect：(A) 彫刻家　(B) 建築家　(C) 技術者
37. firm：(A) 会社　(B) 農場　(C) 牧場
38. based in：(A) 〜に埋まっている　(B) 〜に基づいた
　　　　　　(C) 〜を本拠地とする
39. direction：(A) 引き算　(B) 道案内　(C) 管理
40. whatsoever：(A) いつまでも　(B) 少しも　(C) たくさん

41. career：(A) 運搬機　(B) リヤカー　(C) 職業
42. risk：(A) 後悔　(B) 予測　(C) リスク
43. even so：(A) たとえそうだとしても　(B) 公平に　(C) もしそうなら
44. saying：(A) 〜という　(B) 〜を話す　(C) 話しながら
45. quit：(A) かなりの　(B) 静かな　(C) 〜を辞める
46. current：(A) 通貨　(B) 現在の　(C) 過去の
47. moonlight：(A) 夜間のアルバイトをする　(B) 満月　(C) 夜行性
48. overall：(A) 平均的な　(B) すべてを含めた　(C) 〜を乗り越えて
49. income：(A) 訪問　(B) 売上　(C) 収入
50. creative：(A) 活動的な　(B) 創造的な　(C) 破壊的な

チェックテスト解答

1. **(A)**	2. **(C)**	3. **(C)**	4. **(A)**	5. **(B)**
6. **(B)**	7. **(A)**	8. **(C)**	9. **(A)**	10. **(A)**
11. **(C)**	12. **(B)**	13. **(A)**	14. **(B)**	15. **(B)**
16. **(C)**	17. **(C)**	18. **(A)**	19. **(A)**	20. **(B)**
21. **(B)**	22. **(C)**	23. **(A)**	24. **(C)**	25. **(B)**
26. **(C)**	27. **(C)**	28. **(A)**	29. **(B)**	30. **(C)**
31. **(A)**	32. **(C)**	33. **(C)**	34. **(A)**	35. **(B)**
36. **(B)**	37. **(A)**	38. **(C)**	39. **(B)**	40. **(B)**
41. **(C)**	42. **(C)**	43. **(A)**	44. **(A)**	45. **(C)**
46. **(B)**	47. **(A)**	48. **(B)**	49. **(C)**	50. **(B)**

＜ワンポイント＞

　第3週のトレーニングはいかがでしたか？　ナチュラルスピードのリスニングに慣れてきましたか？　少し耳がなじんできた気がしたら、「リラックスして聞く」ことができ始めている証拠です。でも、耳はなじんできたけれど、「リーディングでは、知らない単語が多くて理解できない」という方も多いはずです。

　実は、リーディング上達のコツは、「知らない単語は無視すること」です。リスニングでは、知らない単語は聞き取れませんから、自然に無視しているのですが、リーディングでは、知らない単語が目に飛び込んできてしまいます。これを無視して、目を先に進めることがポイントです。

　もちろん、復習の際に、知らない単語の意味を確認するのはいいことですが、問題を解く際に気にするのは NG です。知らない単語に意識を向けるのではなく、知っている単語から想像しましょう。リスニング力同様、リーディング力も想像力です。

第 5 章

Week 4

Week 4
今週のトレーニング

Day 1〜 Day 5 のトレーニング		
Step	内容	時間
1	リスニング問題（3問）	2分
2	リーディング問題（3問）	3分
3	文法・語彙問題（5問）	2分
4	解答・解説チェック	3分
5	直読直解トレーニング ① CD（英語）を聞いて、英文を目で追う。 ② CD（英語）を聞いて、日本語訳を目で追う。 ③ カンマ (,)、ピリオド (.)、スラッシュ (/) の単位で、英文の意味が理解できるか確認（理解できない部分は、日本語訳や語彙を参照）。	5〜15分
6	基本構文トレーニング ① 1文ずつCD（日本語・英語）を聞き、英語を数回音読。 ② 10文の英語を続けて音読（数回行なう）。 ③ テキストを縦に半分に折るなどして日本語訳を隠し、英語部分を見て意味がすぐにわかるか確認。 ④ 応用トレーニング「ルックアップ＆セイ」「音読筆写」「リピーティング」	5〜15分

＜ワンポイント＞

　移動中などに、音声CDを使って「基本構文のシャドウイング」（12ページ）を、試してみましたか？　うまくできないという方は、応用トレーニングに「リピーティング」を加えると、シャドウイングが楽になるはずです。

リピーティング	基本構文（日→英）を聞き、英語のあとで一時停止して、何も見ずに聞き取った英語を話します。

Day 1 説明文トレーニング

Step 1 リスニング問題
CDを聞いて、問題を解こう。＜制限時間2分＞

Q1. Who will find the talk the most interesting?
   (A) Parents of very young children
   (B) Parents of teenagers
   (C) University students majoring in music
   (D) Fans of the local symphony

Q2. Which of the following can take a Little Maestros course immediately?
   (A) A five-month-old baby
   (B) A three-year-old girl
   (C) A five-year-old boy
   (D) Twins celebrating their sixth birthday

Q3. What does the talk make clear?
   (A) The children will become professional musicians.
   (B) The children must buy the instruments.
   (C) The children are musical geniuses.
   (D) The children touch the instruments.

Step 2　リーディング問題

英文を読んで、問題を解こう。＜制限時間３分＞

It is said that music helps a young child's brain development. This is why one enterprising community center has introduced the Little Maestros course. In ten sessions, children ages two through four are introduced to musical instruments. They get a hands-on experience with mostly percussion instruments. All teachers are qualified music school graduates. Some are even well-known artists or members of the local symphony. It is all about having fun with music and getting kids used to handling and using musical instruments. The course has become very popular, and there is now a waiting list to get in.

Q4. What is the purpose of the Little Maestros course?
　　(A) To help children enter music school when they are older
　　(B) To train future members of the symphony
　　(C) To get children used to handling musical instruments
　　(D) To help children who have learning problems

Q5. What is true of all the teachers at Little Maestros?
　　(A) They have graduated from music school.
　　(B) They are well-known musicians.
　　(C) They are members of symphony orchestras.
　　(D) They are parents of young children.

Q6. Which of these instruments would probably be used in the Little Maestros course?
　　(A) Organs
　　(B) Drums
　　(C) Harps
　　(D) Flutes

Step 3　文法・語彙問題
空欄にふさわしい語句を選ぼう。＜制限時間2分＞

Q7. Children are introduced ----- musical instruments at an early age.
   (A) in
   (B) to
   (C) at
   (D) on

Q8. They get a ----- experience with percussion instruments and learn to play them.
   (A) handle
   (B) hands-off
   (C) handout
   (D) hands-on

Q9. In that school, all teachers are qualified music school -----.
   (A) graduates
   (B) graduating
   (C) to graduate
   (D) graduated from

Q10. It is ----- about having fun with music and getting used to instruments.
   (A) everyone   (B) total
   (C) all   (D) complete

Q11. Because the course is so popular, there is now a waiting ----- to get in.
   (A) record
   (B) roll
   (C) file
   (D) list

Step 4　解答・解説チェック
現時点での理解度を確認しよう。

問題文は、子供たちのための音楽教室の話です。

1. 正解 **(A)**。質問：「この話にもっとも関心を持つのは、誰ですか？」。答え：「幼い子供がいる保護者」。ヒント：It is said that music helps a young child's brain development.
2. 正解 **(B)**。質問：「すぐにリトルマエストロズ・コースを受講できるのは、次のうち誰ですか？」。答え：「3歳の少女」。ヒント：In ten sessions, children ages two through four are introduced to musical instruments.
3. 正解 **(D)**。質問：「この話で明らかなことは、何ですか？」。答え：「子供たちが、楽器に触れる」。ヒント：It is all about having fun with music and getting kids used to handling and using musical instruments.
4. 正解 **(C)**。質問：「リトルマエストロズ・コースの主な目的は、何ですか？」。答え：「子供たちを楽器の扱いに慣れさせること」。ヒント：It is all about having fun with music and getting kids used to handling and using musical instruments.
5. 正解 **(A)**。質問：「リトルマエストロズのすべての指導者たちに関して、正しい記述はどれですか？」。答え：「音楽学校を卒業している」。ヒント：All teachers are qualified music school graduates.
6. 正解 **(B)**。質問：「リトルマエストロズ・コースで使用されると思われる楽器は、次のどれですか？」。答え：「ドラム」。ヒント：They get a hands-on experience with mostly percussion instruments.
7. 正解 **(B)**。to を選び、be introduced to「～が紹介される」を完成させる。
8. 正解 **(D)**。文意から、hands-on experience「実際に自分でやってみる体験」を完成させる。
9. 正解 **(A)**。文意から、graduates「卒業生」（複数形）を選ぶ。
10. 正解 **(C)**。文意から、it is all about + 動詞 ing「～をすることが目的のすべて」を完成させる。
11. 正解 **(D)**。文意から、waiting list「順番待ちのリスト」を完成させる。

Step 5　直読直解トレーニング

速読速聴力を高めよう。

(※日本語訳は、英語の原文の順序どおりに記してあります。)

It is said / that music helps / a young child's brain development.
いわれます、音楽は助けると、幼児の脳の発達を。
This is why / one enterprising community center / has introduced /
というわけで、ある意欲的なコミュニティ・センターが、導入しました、
the Little Maestros course. In ten sessions, children /
リトルマエストロズ・コースを。10回のセッションで、子供たちに、
ages two through four / are introduced to musical instruments.
2歳から4歳の、楽器が紹介されます。
They get a hands-on experience / with mostly percussion instruments.
彼らは体験します、主に打楽器を。
All teachers are / qualified music school graduates. Some are even /
すべての指導者は、資格を持った音楽学校卒業生です。中には、〜さえいます、
well-known artists or members of the local symphony. It is all about /
著名なアーティストや地元オーケストラのメンバー。それは〜に尽きます、
having fun with music / and getting kids used to / handling and using /
音楽を楽しみ、子供たちを慣れさせる、取り扱うことに、
musical instruments. The course has become very popular,
楽器を。このコースは非常に人気になっています、
and there is now a waiting list / to get in.
そして今では順番待ちがあります、受講のための。

語句

- **brain**：脳
- **instrument**：楽器
- **qualified**：資格のある
- **well-known**：著名な
- **used to**：〜に慣れている
- **enterprising**：意欲的な
- **percussion**：打楽器
- **graduate**：卒業生
- **symphony**：交響楽団
- **handle**：〜を扱う

Step 6　基本構文トレーニング
文法・語彙力を高めよう。

151	音楽は幼児の脳の発達を助けます。	Music helps a young child's brain development.
152	あるコミュニティ・センターが、そのコースを導入しました。	One community center has introduced the course.
153	子供たちに、楽器が紹介されます。	Children are introduced to musical instruments.
154	彼らは、打楽器を体験します。	They get a hands-on experience with percussion instruments.
155	すべての指導者は、資格を持った音楽学校卒業生です。	All teachers are qualified music school graduates.
156	中には、著名なアーティストさえもいます。	Some are even well-known artists.
157	彼らは、地元オーケストラのメンバーです。	They are members of the local symphony.
158	それは、音楽を楽しむことに尽きます。	It is all about having fun with music.
159	そのコースは非常に人気になっています。	The course has become very popular.
160	今では、受講のための順番待ちがあります。	There is now a waiting list to get in.

Week 4

Day 2 会話文トレーニング

Step 1　リスニング問題
CD を聞いて、問題を解こう。＜制限時間 2 分＞

Q1. Who are the speakers?
　　(A) A father and daughter
　　(B) A husband and wife
　　(C) A pilot and flight attendant
　　(D) A doctor and nurse

Q2. On Sunday where will the woman be?
　　(A) On vacation
　　(B) On a Train
　　(C) At work
　　(D) In a plane

Q3. How many tickets were changed?
　　(A) One
　　(B) Two
　　(C) Three
　　(D) Four

Step 2　リーディング問題
英文を読んで、問題を解こう。＜制限時間3分＞

W: So are we going to have to rebook our flights?
M: Maybe. I now have to be back by the 11th. That's the day we were supposed to fly back.

W: It's going to cost us an extra $100 on each ticket to change these flights. Why don't we do this: leave our flight as is and I'll fly back with the kids that day.
M: OK, and then I'll just fly out a day early. That may be a good idea.
W: I think it'll work. What's one day? Nothing really.

W: So was it possible to do it that way?
M: Yes, I'm flying back on Saturday and you guys on Sunday.

Q4. Why are the man and woman talking about changing their plans?
　　(A) Because their airline might go on strike
　　(B) Because the man must go back a day earlier
　　(C) Because their original flights have been cancelled
　　(D) Because they can get a $100 discount if they leave early

Q5. When the conversation ends, how many flights have they rebooked?
　　(A) One
　　(B) Two
　　(C) Three
　　(D) Four

Q6. What day of the week is the 11th?
　　(A) Friday　　　　　　　(B) Saturday
　　(C) Sunday　　　　　　 (D) Monday

Step 3　文法・語彙問題
空欄にふさわしい語句を選ぼう。＜制限時間2分＞

Q7. Are we going to ----- rebook our flights for the return trip?
 (A) should
 (B) must
 (C) have to
 (D) ought to

Q8. I have to be back ----- the 11th because I have a meeting that day.
 (A) in
 (B) until
 (C) while
 (D) by

Q9. That's the day we were ----- to fly back, on our original schedule.
 (A) suppose
 (B) supposed
 (C) to suppose
 (D) supposing

Q10. It's going to ----- us an extra $100 if we change the flight.
 (A) price
 (B) value
 (C) cost
 (D) spend

Q11. You get an earlier flight, but leave our flight -----.
 (A) as is
 (B) is as
 (C) as it
 (D) it is

Step 4　解答・解説チェック

現時点での理解度を確認しよう。

問題文は、旅行先から帰る飛行機の予約の変更について話す男女の会話です。

1. 正解 **(B)**。質問：「話し手たちは、どんな人ですか？」。答え：「夫婦」。ヒント：and I'll fly back with the kids that day.
2. 正解 **(D)**。質問：「日曜日に、女性はどこにいますか？」。答え：「飛行機の中」。ヒント：I'm flying back on Saturday and you guys on Sunday.
3. 正解 **(A)**。質問：「変更になったチケットは、何枚ですか？」。答え：「1枚」。ヒント：I'll just fly out a day early.
4. 正解 **(B)**。質問：「この男性と女性は、なぜ予定を変更することを話し合っていますか？」。答え：「男性が1日早く帰らなくてはならないから」。ヒント：I now have to be back by the 11th. That's the day..., I'll just fly out a day early.
5. 正解 **(A)**。質問：「会話の終わりで、彼らはいくつの便を再予約しましたか？」。答え：「1便」。ヒント：I'm flying back on Saturday and you guys on Sunday.
6. 正解 **(C)**。質問：「11日は、何曜日ですか？」。答え：「日曜日」。ヒント：by the 11th. That's the day we were supposed to fly back., and you guys on Sunday.
7. 正解 **(C)**。選択肢は、be going to のあとなので動詞の原形がくる。have to を選ぶ。
8. 正解 **(D)**。文意から、行為の完了の時点を示す前置詞 by「〜までに（は）」を選ぶ。（B）は行為の継続の終了時を示して、「〜まで（ずっと）」。
9. 正解 **(B)**。文意から、be supposed to + 動詞「〜することになっている」の過去形を完成させる。
10. 正解 **(C)**。文意から、cost +（人）+（費用）「（人）に（費用）がかかる」を完成させる。
11. 正解 **(A)**。文意から、leave 〜 as is「〜をそのままにしておく」を完成させる。

Step 5 　直読直解トレーニング
速読速聴力を高めよう。

（※日本語訳は、英語の原文の順序どおりに記してあります。）

W: So / are we going to have to / rebook our flights?
では、われわれはしないといけないのですか、飛行機の便の再予約を？

M: Maybe. I now have to be back / by the 11th.
たぶんそうです。戻らないといけなくなりました、11日までに。
That's the day / we were supposed to fly back.
それは日です、われわれが帰りの便に乗ることになっていた。

W: It's going to cost us / an extra $100 / on each ticket /
それでわれわれに費用がかかります、100ドル余計に、それぞれのチケットに、
to change these flights. Why don't we do this: leave our flight as is /
便を変更するために。こうしましょう。飛行機の便はこのままにして、
and I'll fly back / with the kids that day.
私は帰りの便に乗ります、その日に子供たちと。

M: OK, and then / I'll just fly out a day early. That may be a good idea.
はい、それで、私は1日早く飛行機に乗ります。いい考えかもしれません。

W: I think / it'll work. What's one day? Nothing really.
思います、うまくいくと。1日くらいかまいません。なんでもありません。

W: So / was it possible / to do it that way?
それで、可能でしたか、そのようにすることは？

M: Yes, I'm flying back / on Saturday / and you guys on Sunday.
はい、帰りの便に乗ります、土曜日に、そしてあなたたちは日曜日に。

語句		
rebook：〜を再予約する		**be supposed to**：〜することになっている
cost：〜に費用がかかる		**extra**：追加の
leave：〜をそのままにしておく		**as is**：現状のまま
fly out：飛行機で発つ		**work**：うまくいく
possible：可能な		**you guys**：君たち

Step 6 基本構文トレーニング

文法・語彙力を高めよう。

161	われわれは、飛行機の便の再予約をしないといけないのですか？	Are we going to have to rebook our flights?
162	11日までに戻らないといけなくなりました。	I now have to be back by the 11th.
163	それは、われわれが帰りの便に乗ることになっていた日です。	That's the day we were supposed to fly back.
164	それで、われわれに100ドル余計に費用がかかります。	It's going to cost us an extra $100.
165	われわれの便はこのままにしておきましょう。	Leave our flight as is.
166	その日に子供たちと帰りの便に乗ります。	I'll fly back with the kids that day.
167	1日早く飛行機に乗ります。	I'll just fly out a day early.
168	それは、うまくいくと思います。	I think it'll work.
169	そのようにすることは、可能でしたか？	Was it possible to do it that way?
170	私は、土曜日に帰りの便に乗ります。	I'm flying back on Saturday.

Day 3　説明文トレーニング

Step 1　リスニング問題
CDを聞いて、問題を解こう。＜制限時間2分＞

Q1. Why are stores crowded after December 25?
　　(A) People are returning unwanted Christmas gifts.
　　(B) People are looking for bargains.
　　(C) People are getting ready for the New Year holidays.
　　(D) People are preparing in case bad weather hits.

Q2. Which of the following attracts the most visitors?
　　(A) Small malls
　　(B) Large malls
　　(C) Local shops
　　(D) Ethnic neighborhoods

Q3. What reduces the number of shoppers?
　　(A) Bad weather
　　(B) Heavy traffic
　　(C) School vacations
　　(D) Road construction

Step 2 リーディング問題

英文を読んで、問題を解こう。＜制限時間3分＞

Once Christmas is over, the bargain sales begin. The problem is that everyone knows this, and it can be a battle to compete with the crowds. There are ways to avoid the hassles of large crowds while still getting the bargains. Avoid the large malls and stick to the strip malls or local shops. For high-end goods, get there early the first day they open. Bargains are snapped up quickly at these places, so be fast. Also, hope that it rains. People tend to put off shopping or head to the indoor malls when it rains. That way, you can beat the crowds to the punch.

Q4. What are these tips for?
　（A）Buying gifts
　（B）Going shopping
　（C）Enjoying holidays
　（D）Selling unwanted items

Q5. According to the advice here, which of these would be an advantage?
　（A）Going to a large mall when it is raining
　（B）Going to a small local shop when the weather is good
　（C）Going to a sale of high-end goods just before Christmas
　（D）Going to a strip mall on a rainy day

Q6. What is the biggest problem mentioned in the passage?
　（A）Prices
　（B）Crowds
　（C）Weather
　（D）Holidays

Step 3　文法・語彙問題

空欄にふさわしい語句を選ぼう。＜制限時間2分＞

Q7. It can be a battle to compete ----- the crowds at bargain sales.
　　(A) to
　　(B) out
　　(C) with
　　(D) of

Q8. There are ways to ----- the hassles of crowds at sales.
　　(A) avoid
　　(B) fail
　　(C) compete
　　(D) direct

Q9. ----- to the strip malls or local shops and stay away from large malls.
　　(A) Stuck
　　(B) Stick
　　(C) Sticking
　　(D) To stick

Q10. Go on a rainy day because people tend to put -----shopping when it rains.
　　(A) out　　　　　　　　(B) on
　　(C) over　　　　　　　(D) off

Q11. You can beat the crowds to the ----- if you follow these tips.
　　(A) push
　　(B) punch
　　(C) pull
　　(D) patch

Step 4　解答・解説チェック

現時点での理解度を確認しよう。

問題文は、バーゲンセールをうまく活用するためのヒントです。

1. 正解 **(B)**。質問：「12月25日以降、店が混雑するのはなぜですか？」。答え：「人びとがバーゲンを探しているため」。ヒント：Once Christmas is over, the bargain sales begin. The problem is that everyone knows this, and it can be a battle to compete with the crowds.
2. 正解 **(B)**。質問：「ほとんどの客が魅力を感じるのは、次のどれですか？」。答え：「大規模なモール」。ヒント：There are ways to avoid the hassles of large crowds while still getting the bargains. Avoid the large malls...
3. 正解 **(A)**。質問：「買い物客の数を減らしてしまう原因は、何ですか？」。答え：「悪天候」。ヒント：People tend to put off shopping or head to the indoor malls when it rains.
4. 正解 **(B)**。質問：「これらは、何のヒントですか？」。答え：「買い物に行く」。ヒント：There are ways to avoid the hassles of large crowds while still getting the bargains.
5. 正解 **(D)**。質問：「アドバイスによると、得することは次のどれですか？」。答え：「雨の日に小規模ショッピングセンターに行く」。ヒント：stick to the strip malls or local shops., hope that it rains.
6. 正解 **(B)**。質問：「文書に述べられている、最大の問題は何ですか？」。答え：「人ごみ」。ヒント：There are ways to avoid the hassles of large crowds
7. 正解 **(C)**。文意から、compete with「～と競い合う」を完成させる。
8. 正解 **(A)**。選択肢はすべて動詞。文意から、avoid「～を避ける」を選ぶ。
9. 正解 **(B)**。主語がないので、動詞で始まる命令文。Stick（動詞・原形）を選び、stick to「～に固執する」を完成させる。
10. 正解 **(D)**。put off + 名詞（相当語句）「～を延期する」を完成させる。
11. 正解 **(B)**。beat ～ to the punch「～の先を越す」を完成させる。

Step 5　直読直解トレーニング

速読速聴力を高めよう。

(※日本語訳は、英語の原文の順序どおりに記してあります。)

Once Christmas is over, the bargain sales begin. The problem is /
クリスマスが終わるとすぐに、バーゲンセールが始まります。問題は、
that everyone knows this, and it can be a battle / to compete with /
誰もがこのことを知っていて、戦いになりかねないことです、競う、
the crowds. There are ways / to avoid the hassles / of large crowds /
大勢の人と。方法があります、わずらわしさを避ける、人ごみの、
while still getting the bargains. Avoid the large malls / and stick to /
お買い得品を手に入れながらも。大型モールを避けて、執着しましょう、
the strip malls / or local shops. For high-end goods, get there early /
小規模モールや、地元商店に。高級品に関しては、早い時間に出向きましょう、
the first day they open. Bargains are snapped up quickly / at these places,
開店初日の。お買い得品はすぐに買われてしまいます、こうした場所では、
so be fast. Also, hope that it rains. People tend to /
ですから急ぎましょう。また、雨を期待しましょう。人びとは〜しがちです、
put off shopping / or head to the indoor malls / when it rains.
買い物を先延ばしに、あるいは屋内モールに向かいます、雨が降ると。
That way, you can beat the crowds to the punch.
そうすれば、人ごみの先を越すことができるでしょう。

語句

- **once**：〜するやいなや
- **crowd**：群衆
- **strip mall**：小規模モール
- **snap up**：〜に飛びつく
- **head to**：〜に向かう
- **battle**：戦い
- **hassle**：面倒なこと
- **high-end**：最高級の
- **tend to**：〜しがちである
- **indoor**：屋内の

Step 6　基本構文トレーニング
文法・語彙力を高めよう。

171	問題は、誰もがこのことを知っていることです。	The problem is that everyone knows this.
172	それは、大勢の人と競う戦いになりかねません。	It can be a battle to compete with the crowds.
173	わずらわしさを避ける方法があります。	There are ways to avoid the hassles.
174	大型モールを避けてください。	Avoid the large malls.
175	小規模モールや地元商店に執着しましょう。	Stick to the strip malls or local shops.
176	開店初日の早い時間に出向きましょう。	Get there early the first day they open.
177	こうした場所では、お買い得品はすぐに買われてしまいます。	Bargains are snapped up quickly at these places.
178	雨が降ることを期待しましょう。	Hope that it rains.
179	雨が降ると、人びとは買い物を先延ばしにしがちです。	People tend to put off shopping when it rains.
180	人ごみの先を越すことができるでしょう。	You can beat the crowds to the punch.

Day 4　会話文トレーニング

Step 1　リスニング問題
CDを聞いて、問題を解こう。＜制限時間2分＞

Q1. What happened first?
　　(A) Gerald picked up his camera.
　　(B) Gerald heard a noise.
　　(C) Gerald started shooting.
　　(D) Gerald talked to Pamela.

Q2. Which of the following does the conversation make clear?
　　(A) Where Gerald lives
　　(B) What Gerald does
　　(C) Whether Gerald is married
　　(D) How old Gerald is

Q3. Why did Pamela talk to Gerald?
　　(A) He is a well-known local police officer.
　　(B) He stopped a bomb from exploding.
　　(C) He saw something important happen.
　　(D) He is a famous politician.

Step 2 リーディング問題

英文を読んで、問題を解こう。＜制限時間 3 分＞

W: This is Pamela Wesley, WSSK News, live from the scene talking here with Gerald Hasselbeck. Gerald, you saw the whole scene unfold in front of you.
M: Yes, I did. I live up there in that building on the tenth floor.

W: So what was your reaction when you heard the boom?
M: At first I thought it was a bomb. It was that loud. Then I looked out and started shooting.
W: Now, check out some of that amazing video Mr. Hasselbeck here shot.

W: How were you able to hold that camera so steady? Weren't you shaken up?
M: I don't know. I just pointed and shot.

Q4. Who is Pamela Wesley?
　　(A) A photographer　　　　(B) A newspaper writer
　　(C) A TV news reporter　　(D) A radio news reporter

Q5. Where is this conversation taking place?
　　(A) Just outside Mr. Hasselbeck's home
　　(B) At the WSSK studio
　　(C) On the tenth floor of a building
　　(D) At the location of a bomb explosion

Q6. What did Mr. Hasselbeck pick up soon after he heard a noise?
　　(A) A gun　　　　　　　(B) A video camera
　　(C) A phone　　　　　　(D) His glasses

Step 3　文法・語彙問題
空欄にふさわしい語句を選ぼう。＜制限時間2分＞

Q7. You saw the whole ----- unfold in front of you when it happened, didn't you?
　　(A) seen　　　　　　(B) sign
　　(C) science　　　　　(D) scene

Q8. What was your ----- when you heard the boom?
　　(A) reaction
　　(B) react
　　(C) reacted
　　(D) reacting

Q9. ----- first I thought it was a bomb, but I wasn't sure.
　　(A) The
　　(B) My
　　(C) At
　　(D) On

Q10. I looked out and started ----- with my video camera.
　　(A) taking
　　(B) seeing
　　(C) spotting
　　(D) shooting

Q11. Weren't you shaken ----- by seeing the accident?
　　(A) over
　　(B) up
　　(C) down
　　(D) back

Step 4　解答・解説チェック

現時点での理解度を確認しよう。

問題文は、爆発の現場を目撃した人への取材です。

1. 正解 **(B)**。質問：「最初に、何が起こりましたか？」。答え：「ジェラルドが騒音を聞いた」。ヒント：what was your reaction when you heard the boom?
2. 正解 **(A)**。質問：「この会話で明らかなのは、次のどれですか？」。答え：「ジェラルドがどこに住んでいるか」。ヒント：I live up there in that building on the tenth floor.
3. 正解 **(C)**。質問：「パメラは、なぜジェラルドに声をかけたのですか？」。答え：「彼が、何か重要なことが起こったのを見たから」。ヒント：Gerald, you saw the whole scene unfold in front of you.
4. 正解 **(C)**。質問：「パメラ・ウェズリーは、どんな人ですか？」。答え：「テレビのレポーター」。ヒント：This is Pamela Wesley, WSSK News,
5. 正解 **(A)**。質問：「この会話は、どこで行なわれていますか？」。答え：「ハッセルベック氏の家のすぐ外」。ヒント：I live up there in that building
6. 正解 **(B)**。質問：「騒音を聞いた直後にハッセルベック氏が手にしたものは、何でしたか？」。答え：「ビデオカメラ」。ヒント：Then I looked out and started shooting.
7. 正解 **(D)**。文意から、whole scene「（初めから終わりまで）すべて」を完成させる。
8. 正解 **(A)**。指示代名詞 your のあとなので名詞がくる。reaction「反応」を選ぶ。(B)「〜に反応する」（動詞）、(C) 動詞過去形、(D)「反応すること」（動名詞）。
9. 正解 **(C)**。文意から、at first「最初は」を完成させる。
10. 正解 **(D)**。start + 動詞 ing で、「〜し始める」。文意から、shooting「撮影すること」を選ぶ。
11. 正解 **(B)**。文意から、be shaken up「動揺した」を完成させる。

Week 4

Step 5　直読直解トレーニング

速読速聴力を高めよう。

(※日本語訳は、英語の原文の順序どおりに記してあります。)

W:　This is Pamela Wesley, WSSK News, live from the scene /
　　パメラ・ウェズリーです、WSSK ニュースの、現場からの中継で、
　　talking here / with Gerald Hasselbeck.
　　ここで話しています、ジェラルド・ハッセルベック氏と。
　　Gerald, you saw the whole scene / unfold in front of you.
　　ジェラルド、あなたは一部始終を目撃しました、目の前で起こった。

M:　Yes, I did. I live up there / in that building / on the tenth floor.
　　はい、見ました。私はそこに住んでいます、あのビルの、10 階に。

W:　So / what was your reaction / when you heard the boom?
　　それで、あなたの印象はどうでしたか、爆発音を聞いた時?

M:　At first / I thought / it was a bomb. It was that loud.
　　最初は、思いました、それが爆弾だと。それほど大きい音でした。
　　Then / I looked out / and started shooting.
　　それから、外を見て、撮影し始めました。

W:　Now, check out / some of that amazing video /
　　では、ご覧ください、驚くべき映像の一部を、
　　Mr. Hasselbeck here shot.
　　ハッセルベック氏が撮った。

W:　How were you able to / hold that camera / so steady?
　　どうしてできたのですか、カメラを持つことが、そんなにしっかりと?
　　Weren't you shaken up?
　　動揺しなかったのですか?

M:　I don't know. I just pointed and shot.
　　わかりません。カメラを向けて撮っただけです。

語句
unfold：場面が展開する　**in front of**：〜の前に　**reaction**：反応
boom：ドーンという音　**that**：それほど　**look out**：外を見る　**shoot**：〜を撮影する
check out：〜を確かめる　**amazing**：驚くべき　**steady**：しっかりとした

Step 6　基本構文トレーニング
文法・語彙力を高めよう。

181	あなたは、目の前ですべてを目撃しました。	You saw the whole scene unfold in front of you.
182	私は、あそこのあのビルに住んでいます。	I live up there in that building.
183	爆発音を聞いた時、あなたの印象はどうでしたか？	What was your reaction when you heard the boom?
184	最初は、それが爆弾だと思いました。	At first I thought it was a bomb.
185	それは、それほど大きい音でした。	It was that loud.
186	外を見て、撮影し始めました。	I looked out and started shooting.
187	彼が撮った、驚くべき映像の一部をご覧ください。	Check out some of that amazing video he shot.
188	どうしてそんなにしっかりとカメラを持っていられたのですか？	How were you able to hold that camera so steady?
189	動揺しなかったのですか？	Weren't you shaken up?
190	カメラを向けて撮っただけです。	I just pointed and shot.

Day 5 説明文トレーニング

Step 1　リスニング問題
CDを聞いて、問題を解こう。＜制限時間2分＞

Q1. How does Houghton and Powell view neckties?
   (A) As worthless in the office
   (B) As necessary on some days
   (C) As more fashionable than bowties
   (D) As essential for managers

Q2. Who would probably dislike the information?
   (A) Makers of neckties
   (B) People who like to dress casually
   (C) Employees fond of shorts and sandals
   (D) The new CEO at Houghton and Powell

Q3. How often can Houghton and Powell employees go to work in sandals?
   (A) Every day
   (B) Once a month
   (C) Once a week
   (D) Every other day

Step 2 リーディング問題

英文を読んで、問題を解こう。＜制限時間3分＞

The necktie is such a standard of business attire yet such an unnecessary part of clothing. This is why one business is abandoning the necktie. It's no longer part of their unofficial "office uniform." Houghton and Powell Enterprises have actually ordered all their male employees to abandon the necktie. They have adopted a more casual approach to office attire. Even their Casual Fridays go far beyond the usual norm, and employees are allowed to wear shorts, sandals, and T-shirts. Why the change? It's all part of their new CEO's laid-back outlook on business and life. There's no word yet on whether the bowtie has been abandoned at Houghton and Powell.

Q4. What does this passage refer to?
 (A) Neckties worn outside the office
 (B) Business attire for men in an office
 (C) Shops that sell casual work clothes
 (D) Clothes for men and women at work

Q5. What is true of Houghton and Powell Enterprises?
 (A) Bowties are not permitted in the office.
 (B) No employees should wear shorts and sandals at work.
 (C) Women can wear whatever they want to wear at work.
 (D) Male employees should not wear neckties in the office.

Q6. What is said about Casual Fridays at Houghton and Powell?
 (A) They are not popular.
 (B) They have been abandoned.
 (C) They have just been started.
 (D) They are more casual than usual.

Step 3　文法・語彙問題

空欄にふさわしい語句を選ぼう。＜制限時間2分＞

Q7. The necktie is ----- a standard of business attire.
　　(A) so
　　(B) very
　　(C) such
　　(D) many

Q8. It's unnecessary, so this is ----- one business is abandoning the necktie.
　　(A) what
　　(B) why
　　(C) that
　　(D) reason

Q9. They ordered their male employees ----- the necktie.
　　(A) abandon
　　(B) to abandon
　　(C) abandoned
　　(D) abandoning

Q10. Under the new policy, Casual Fridays go far beyond the usual -----.
　　(A) normal
　　(B) normality
　　(C) norm
　　(D) normalcy

Q11. There's no ----- on whether the bowtie has been abandoned.
　　(A) speaking
　　(B) saying
　　(C) paper
　　(D) word

Step 4　解答・解説チェック
現時点での理解度を確認しよう。

問題文は、オフィスでのカジュアルな服装についての話です。

1. 正解 **(A)**。質問：「ハウトン・アンド・パウエルの、ネクタイに関する見解はどうですか？」。答え：「オフィスでは無用の物である」。ヒント：ordered all their male employees to abandon the necktie.
2. 正解 **(A)**。質問：「情報を気に入らないと思われるのは、誰ですか？」。答え：「ネクタイ製造者」。ヒント：This is why one business is abandoning the necktie.
3. 正解 **(C)**。質問：「ハウトン・アンド・パウエルの従業員が、サンダルで出社できる頻度は、どれくらいですか？」。答え：「週1回」。ヒント：employees are allowed to wear shorts, sandals, and T-shirts.
4. 正解 **(B)**。質問：「この文書は、何についてのものですか？」。答え：「オフィスでの男性の服装」。ヒント：The necktie is such a standard of business attire
5. 正解 **(D)**。質問：「ハウトン・アンド・パウエル・エンタープライゼズに関して、正しい記述は何ですか？」。答え：「男性社員は、オフィスでネクタイを着用してはいけない」。ヒント：Houghton and Powell Enterprises have actually ordered all their male employees to abandon the necktie.
6. 正解 **(D)**。質問：「ハウトン・アンド・パウエルでのカジュアル・フライデーに関して、どんなことが言われていますか？」。答え：「一般的なものよりカジュアルである」。ヒント：They have adopted a more casual approach to office attire.
7. 正解 **(C)**。文意から、名詞を強調する such を選ぶ。（A）（B）は、形容詞・副詞を強調する。（D）は、複数名詞を修飾して「たくさんの」。
8. 正解 **(B)**。this is why + 節「これが、〜の理由である」を完成させる。
9. 正解 **(B)**。文意から、order +（人）+ to + 動詞「（人）に〜するよう命じる」の過去形を完成させる。
10. 正解 **(C)**。文意から、usual norm「一般的な基準」を完成させる。
11. 正解 **(D)**。there's no word on「〜についての言及はない」を完成させる。

Step 5　直読直解トレーニング

速読速聴力を高めよう。

（※日本語訳は、英語の原文の順序どおりに記してあります。）

The necktie is / such a standard of business attire /
ネクタイは、まさにビジネスウェアのスタンダードです、
yet such an unnecessary part of clothing. This is why / one business /
衣服にまったく不必要な部分ですが。これが理由です、ある企業が、
is abandoning the necktie. It's no longer / part of / their unofficial /
ネクタイを廃止している。もはやありません、一部では、彼らの非公式な
"office uniform." Houghton and Powell Enterprises /
「職場の制服」の。ハウトン・アンド・パウエル・エンタープライゼズは、
have actually ordered / all their male employees / to abandon the necktie.
実際に指示しました、男性社員全員に、ネクタイをやめるように。
They have adopted / a more casual approach / to office attire.
彼らは採用しました、よりカジュアルな取り組みを、オフィスの服装として。
Even their Casual Fridays / go far beyond the usual norm,
彼らのカジュアル・フライデーもまた、一般的な基準をはるかに超えています、
and employees are allowed / to wear / shorts, sandals, and T-shirts.
従業員は許されています、着用することが、短パン、サンダル、Tシャツを。
Why the change? It's all part of / their new CEO's laid-back outlook /
なぜ変化が？　それはすべて一端です、新しいCEOのおおらかな見解の、
on business and life. There's no word yet / on whether /
ビジネスと人生に対する。言及はまだありません、〜かどうかについての、
the bowtie has been abandoned / at Houghton and Powell.
蝶ネクタイが廃止になった、ハウトン・アンド・パウエルで。

語句

attire：衣装	unnecessary：不必要な
abandon：〜を廃止する	no longer：もはや〜でない
unofficial：非公式の	go beyond：〜をしのぐ
allow：〜を許す	laid-back：おおらかな
outlook：見解	bowtie：蝶ネクタイ

Step 6 基本構文トレーニング
文法・語彙力を高めよう。

191	ネクタイは、まさにビジネスウェアのスタンダードです。	The necktie is such a standard of business attire.
192	それは、衣服にまったく不必要な部分です。	It's such an unnecessary part of clothing.
193	これが、ある企業がネクタイを廃止している理由です。	This is why one business is abandoning the necktie.
194	それは、もはや彼らの非公式な「職場の制服」の一部ではありません。	It's no longer part of their unofficial "office uniform."
195	彼らは、社員にネクタイをやめるように指示しました。	They ordered their employees to abandon the necktie.
196	彼らは、よりカジュアルな取り組みを採用しました。	They have adopted a more casual approach.
197	カジュアル・フライデーは一般的な基準をはるかに超えています。	Casual Fridays go far beyond the usual norm.
198	従業員は、短パン、サンダル、Tシャツの着用が許されています。	Employees are allowed to wear shorts, sandals, and T-shirts.
199	それは、すべて彼らの新しいCEOのおおらかな見解の一端です。	It's all part of their new CEO's laid-back outlook.
200	蝶ネクタイが廃止になったかどうかについては、言及されていません。	There's no word on whether the bowtie has been abandoned.

Day 6 チェックテスト

ふさわしい語句の意味を選ぼう。＜制限時間5分＞

1. brain：(A) 簡素な　(B) 穀物　(C) 脳
2. enterprising：(A) 入場する　(B) 事業　(C) 意欲的な
3. instrument：(A) 指示　(B) 楽器　(C) 設定
4. percussion：(A) 議論　(B) 打楽器　(C) 座椅子
5. qualified：(A) 資格のある　(B) 上質な　(C) 専任の
6. graduate：(A) グラニュー糖　(B) 次第に　(C) 卒業生
7. well-known：(A) よく学ばれた　(B) 知識の豊富な　(C) 著名な
8. symphony：(A) 交響楽団　(B) 共鳴　(C) 同情
9. used to：(A) 〜を再利用する　(B) 〜に慣れている　(C) 使い古された
10. handle：(A) 〜を束ねる　(B) 揺らす　(C) 〜を扱う

11. rebook：(A) 〜を再予約する　(B) 〜を再出版する　(C) 〜を再度読む
12. be supposed to：(A) 〜してほしい　(B) 〜するかも　(C) 〜することになっている
13. cost：(A) 〜に時間がかかる　(B) 〜に手間がかかる　(C) 〜に費用がかかる
14. extra：(A) その他の　(B) 追加の　(C) 出口の
15. leave：(A) 〜を持って行く　(B) 〜を過ぎる　(C) 〜をそのままにしておく
16. as is：(A) そのとおり　(B) 現在では　(C) 現状のまま
17. fly out：(A) 飛び出す　(B) 飛行機から降りる　(C) 飛行機で発つ
18. work：(A) 現場　(B) うまくいく　(C) 歩く
19. possible：(A) 実現した　(B) 可能な　(C) 通行可能な
20. you guys：(A) 彼ら　(B) 男性諸君　(C) 君たち

21. once：(A) 同時に　(B) 昔々　(C) 〜するやいなや
22. battle：(A) ビン　(B) 戦い　(C) ヤカン

23. crowd：(A) 群衆　(B) 雲　(C) 自負
24. hassle：(A) 〜を元気づける　(B) 面倒なこと　(C) 交渉
25. strip mall：(A) 迷惑メール　(B) 製糸工場　(C) 小規模モール
26. high-end：(A) 売れ残りの　(B) 最高級の　(C) 不良品の
27. snap up：(A) 〜に飛びつく　(B) 速球を投げる　(C) 指を鳴らす
28. tend to：(A) 〜しがちである　(B) 〜しなければならない
　　　　　　 (C) 〜したものである
29. head to：(A) 〜を考える　(B) 〜に向かう　(C) 〜を指揮する
30. indoor：(A) 屋内の　(B) ドアの　(C) 内側に開くドア

31. unfold：(A) 折りたたむ　(B) 〜を中止する　(C) 場面が展開する
32. in front of：(A) 人前で　(B) 〜の前に　(C) 玄関口に
33. reaction：(A) やり直す　(B) 反応　(C) 再反応
34. boom：(A) 発展　(B) 爆発物　(C) ドーンという音
35. that：(A) それほど　(B) あれくらい　(C) すこし
36. look out：(A) 外を見る　(B) 目をそらす　(C) 気にしない
37. shoot：(A) かっこいい　(B) 〜に合格する　(C) 〜を撮影する
38. check out：(A) 〜を確かめる　(B) 〜を選び出す　(C) 〜を追い出す
39. amazing：(A) 楽しみな　(B) 驚くべき　(C) 音楽的な
40. steady：(A) しっかりとした　(B) 学問　(C) ゆるんだ

41. attire：(A) 態度　(B) 衣装　(C) 印象
42. unnecessary：(A) 必要な　(B) 不必要な　(C) 予備の
43. abandon：(A) 〜を失う　(B) 〜を禁止する　(C) 〜を廃止する
44. no longer：(A) すぐに　(B) 〜より長くない　(C) もはや〜でない
45. unofficial：(A) 非公式の　(B) 会社外の　(C) 非常識の
46. go beyond：(A) 〜をしのぐ　(B) 〜のうしろに付く　(C) 後退する
47. allow：(A) 〜を許す　(B) 矢　(C) 〜についていく
48. laid-back：(A) 仰向けの　(B) 裏打ちされた　(C) おおらかな
49. outlook：(A) 外を見る　(B) 見解　(C) 的外れ
50. bowtie：(A) 蝶ネクタイ　(B) 幅広のネクタイ　(C) 礼服用ネクタイ

チェックテスト解答

1. (C)	2. (C)	3. (B)	4. (B)	5. (A)
6. (C)	7. (C)	8. (A)	9. (B)	10. (C)
11. (A)	12. (C)	13. (C)	14. (B)	15. (C)
16. (C)	17. (C)	18. (B)	19. (B)	20. (C)
21. (C)	22. (B)	23. (A)	24. (B)	25. (C)
26. (B)	27. (A)	28. (A)	29. (B)	30. (A)
31. (C)	32. (B)	33. (B)	34. (C)	35. (A)
36. (A)	37. (C)	38. (A)	39. (B)	40. (A)
41. (B)	42. (B)	43. (C)	44. (C)	45. (A)
46. (A)	47. (A)	48. (C)	49. (B)	50. (A)

<ワンポイント>

　第4週のトレーニング、お疲れさまでした。それでは、最後の仕上げとして、第6章で問題形式を最終確認しましょう。本番のTOEICテストでは、この1カ月間の成果が試されるわけですが、「これだけがんばったんだから、絶対に失敗はできない」という気負いは禁物です。

　TOEICテストは、600点クリアをめざされるみなさんから、900点以上をめざす方までの英語運用能力を一度に測定します。ですから、とてもやさしい問題もあれば、むずかしい問題もあります。第1章で確認した重点パート（Part 2, Part 5, Part 7のシングルパッセージ）では3問に2問を確実に正答して、それ以外のパートは2問に1問わかればOKぐらいの「リラックスした気持ち」で臨みましょう。

　こう考えて、リスニングでは、聞き逃した問題をいつまでも引きずることなく、次の問題に集中する。リーディングも、むずかしい問題はあっさり捨てて、次の問題に進む。これが実は、スピード対応能力を測定するTOEICテストで実力を発揮するコツなのです。

第 6 章

最終チェック

第 6 章の使い方

TOEIC® テストの問題形式を確認する 25 問の練習問題（約 15 分）です。第 2 章～第 5 章のトレーニング実施後、TOEIC® テスト受験直前に、問題形式の最終確認と準備に活用しましょう。

Part 1（写真描写問題）

写真を見ながら放送を聞いて、ABCDの英文から写真を適切に描写しているものを選び、答えをマークします。

1.

Ⓐ Ⓑ Ⓒ Ⓓ

2.

Ⓐ Ⓑ Ⓒ Ⓓ

＜ワンポイント＞

　Part 1では、**人や物の状態を表わす表現**を聞き取れるかどうかが試されます。写真の人や物の状態に注意して聞きましょう。Part 1は、600点突破の重点パートです。**80％（10問中8問）の正答**をめざしましょう。

Part 2（応答問題）

質問と、それに対する応答 ABC を聞いて、応答としてふさわしいものを選び、答えをマークします。

3. Mark your answer on your answer sheet.

Ⓐ Ⓑ Ⓒ

4. Mark your answer on your answer sheet.

Ⓐ Ⓑ Ⓒ

5. Mark your answer on your answer sheet.

Ⓐ Ⓑ Ⓒ

＜ワンポイント＞
　Part 2 では、**問いかけの目的（情報収集、確認）**が理解できているかどうかが試されます。質問をよく聞いて理解するようにしましょう。Part 2 は、600点突破の重点パートです。**70%（30問中21問）の正答**をめざしましょう。

Part 3（会話問題）

2人の会話を聞いて、印刷された設問（3問）を解き、答えをマークします。

6. At the beginning of the dialogue, how does the man sound?
   (A) Confused
   (B) Confusing
   (C) Excited
   (D) Exciting

7. What did the woman forget to do?
   (A) Buy her own stapler
   (B) Let the man know she had borrowed something
   (C) Read the note Barry put on her desk
   (D) Close the man's desk drawers

8. At the end of the dialogue, what does the woman agree to do?
   (A) Rearrange the things on the man's desk
   (B) Return the man's staples
   (C) Apologize when she does something wrong
   (D) Communicate better

＜ワンポイント＞

　放送が流れる前に、設問に目を通しておくと、設問の答えを探しながら聞くことができます。600点突破には、**(勘も含めて) 50% (30問中15問) の正答で十分ですから、最低1つ、できれば2つの設問に目を通しておくと余裕**を持って会話を聞くことができます。なお、設問は、Who（誰が）、Where（どこで）、When（いつ）で始まるものが比較的やさしい問題です。

最終チェック

Part 4（説明文問題）

スピーチなどを聞いて、印刷された設問（3問）を解き、答えをマークします。

9. What is one of United Mutual's selling points?
   (A) Cheaper fees for all services
   (B) A more convenient location
   (C) Longer operating hours
   (D) Professional advice at a reasonable cost

10. If someone switches to United Mutual on January 2, what does he or she miss?
    (A) Banking until 8 p.m.
    (B) A gift
    (C) Free checking
    (D) Free online banking

11. Which of the following best describes the ad?
    (A) It is an outline of changes expected at the company after December 31.
    (B) It is a brief history of United Mutual.
    (C) It is an explanation of free checking and free online banking.
    (D) It is a list of advantages of using the bank.

＜ワンポイント＞

　Part 3同様に、放送が流れる前に、設問に目を通しておくと、設問の答えを探しながら聞くことができます。600点突破には、**勘も含めて50％（30問中15問）の正答**で十分ですから、**最低1つ、できれば2つの設問に目を通しておく**と、余裕を持って会話を聞くことができます。なお、設問は、Who（誰が）, Where（どこで）, When（いつ）で始まるものが比較的やさしい問題です。

Part 5（短文穴埋め問題）＜制限時間1分30秒＞

空欄部を埋める語句を選びセンテンスを完成させ、答えをマークします。

12. After checking the laundry, Paula found that the colors -----.
    (A) had run
    (B) running
    (C) runner
    (D) run

13. To ----- matters worse, they cannot do anything until next week.
    (A) produce
    (B) make
    (C) do
    (D) create

14. ----- the company is upgrading its electrical system the day after tomorrow, all offices will remain open.
    (A) As if
    (B) Even though
    (C) Accordingly
    (D) Within

＜ワンポイント＞

　Part 5 では、基本的な語彙・文法を使用できるかが試されます。出題は、**単語の意味の違いを問う問題が 1/3、熟語などの慣用表現が 1/3、基本的な文法が 1/3**（主語と動詞の単数・複数の一致、時制、受動態など）です。600点突破には、**70％（40問中28問）の正答**が目標です。時間をかけすぎると、Part 7（読解問題）を解く時間が不足してしまいます。選択肢を一見して、わかりそうにない問題（単語の意味の違いなど）で時間をかけないようにしましょう。

Part 6 （長文穴埋め問題） ＜制限時間1分30秒＞

3カ所の空欄部を埋める語句を選び文書を完成させ、答えをマークします。

Questions 15–17 refer to the following invitation.

Just one week after Gary Willis announced that he is retiring as Union City treasurer, three people have said they will _____ the

15. (A) run
    (B) seek
    (C) become
    (D) try

office. The latest candidate is Marsha Freeman, currently Union City assistant treasurer, an office she _____ for three years.

16. (A) has held
    (B) holds
    (C) is holding
    (D) had been holding

As assistant treasurer, she has been _____ responsible for

17. (A) the chief
    (B) in chief of
    (C) chief
    (D) chiefly

tax billing and the collection of unpaid taxes. She has also compiled state auditor reports for the past two years.

＜ワンポイント＞

Part 6 では、よりライティングに近い形で出題されますが、内容は Part 5 とほぼ同じです。600点突破には、**65％（12問中8問）の正答**が目標です。

Part 7（読解問題－シングルパッセージ） ＜制限時間３分＞

１つの英文を読んで、設問を解いて、答えをマークします。

Questions 18–20 refer to the following advertisement.

Body by Lorelei
Skincare System for the Working Woman

Botox
Smooth out those frown lines with just a few tiny injections. You'll notice the difference within days with treatments up to three months.
$15 per injection

Massage Therapy
After a total body consultation to determine your massage needs, our experienced professional massage therapists go to work to soothe and treat all your aches and pains.
30 mins.:$70   60 mins.:$110   90 mins.:$150

Microdermabrasion
The best method to remove damaged and dead skin. Fine crystals are vacuumed across the skin to rejuvenate those deep skin tissues.
Back:$170   Neck:$35   Face:$150   Shoulders:$35   Hands:$80

Skin Care
Customized treatments by our skin-care professionals are based on our exclusive body-mapping technique. This allows us to zero in on your problem areas and custom design your treatment.
Facials:$120   Hands & Arms:$80   Scalp massage:$50
Feet:$70   Neck & Shoulders:$100

18. Which treatment would a person with sore muscles likely try?
　(A) Skin care　　　　　　(B) Botox
　(C) Microdermabrasion　　(D) Massage therapy

19. Which treatments are advertised as being specially designed for the individual?
　(A) Skin care and botox
　(B) Massage therapy and skin care
　(C) Skin care and microdermabrasion
　(D) Microdermabrasion and botox

20. Which of the following statements is true?
　(A) Microdermabrasion and skin care are charged according to the part of the body.
　(B) Massage therapy and skin care are charged according to the time.
　(C) Botox and microdermabrasion are charged according to the number of injections.
　(D) Massage therapy and botox are charged according to the medicine.

＜ワンポイント＞

　英文を読む前に、**問題の導入文を見る**と（Questions 18–20 refer to the following **advertisement**.）、どんな種類の英文かがわかります。

> ad →広告（advertisement の省略）、memo →社内連絡文書（ある組織内でやり取りしている文書）、notice →お知らせ（社外など組織外の人に向けた文書）、review →批評（何かに対する評価のコメント）など。

　次に、英文のタイトル（Body by Lorelei ― Skincare System for the Working Woman）や最初の数行を読んで、**何のために書かれた英文か**を把握します。続いて、**設問を読み、その答えを探すように英文を読む**と、読解にかかる時間を短縮できます。Part 7（シングルパッセージ）は、600 点突破の重点パートです。**70％（28 問中 20 問）の正答**をめざしましょう。

Part 7（読解問題－ダブルパッセージ）　＜制限時間5分＞

2つの英文を読み、設問（5問）を解いて、答えをマークします。

Questions 21-25 refer to the following article and e-mail.

YOUR CAR IS YOU
By Adam Bernard

We often assume things when we see what type of car or truck someone drives. This may be stereotyping, but a survey by Wheels magazine proves that "we are what we drive." Overwhelmingly, muscle car and Hummer owners were generally single males, while single females tended to prefer sporty, but more reliable, smaller cars. Sports coupes tended to be driven by more middle-aged men more often single than not. Married men and women with kids in two-car families tended to own the typical SUV or minivan, but their choice of second vehicle ranged widely. Over half owned a family sedan, but a solid 22 percent owned a sports coupe as their second car. If you want to learn more about the survey, go to our Web site and click on my blog or pick up the latest edition of Wheels at your newsstand.

Dear Adam,

Loved the info on cars reflecting a person's personality. Couldn't agree more. My good buddy Simon, who is married with three kids, still can't give up his love of Mustangs. When the company reintroduced the model a few years ago, he was one of the first to buy. I'm not saying he's going through a midlife crisis, but he traded in their four-door family sedan for this sportier vehicle.

Walter Rolfe, New Boston, TX

21. What stereotype about drivers is referred to in the review?
    (A) Men are better drivers than women.
    (B) Income determines the kind of car someone drives.
    (C) Cars give clues to people's identities.
    (D) Young people have more accidents than older people do.

22. Who recently bought a car?
    (A) Walter Rolfe
    (B) Someone mentioned in the review
    (C) Adam Bernard
    (D) Someone mentioned in the e-mail

23. What does the e-mail writer think of the reviewer's opinion?
    (A) He has some doubts.
    (B) He criticizes it.
    (C) He supports it.
    (D) He raises some questions.

24. According to the survey, who is most likely to own a sports car?
    (A) Tom, age 29
    (B) Lisa, age 38
    (C) Jack, age 46
    (D) Nancy and Phil, both age 28

25. How many ways can people obtain more information about the Wheels survey?
    (A) One   (B) Two
    (C) Three   (D) Four

＜ワンポイント＞
　600点突破には、**勘も含めて45％（20問中9問）の正答**で十分ですから、4セット（各5問）からやさしそうな問題を2つずつ選んで、確実に解きましょう。

解答

Part 1

1. Look at the picture marked number 1. 1番の写真を見なさい。
   (A) One woman has a baby on her lap.
      1人の女性が赤ん坊を膝に乗せている。
   (B) The woman on the right has a friendly smile.
      右側の女性は、親しみのある笑顔を向けている。
   (C) Only the baby is looking right at the camera.
      赤ん坊だけが、カメラのほうを向いている。
   (D) The older man is grinning broadly.
      年輩の男性は大笑いをしている。

正解：**(B)**
解説：(A) on one's lap「膝の上に」。(B) on the right「右方向の」。(C) look right at the camera「カメラを直視する」。(D) grin broadly「大笑いをする」。

2. Look at the picture marked number 2. 2番の写真を見なさい。
   (A) Everyone is looking toward the fountain.
      全員が、噴水のほうを見ている。
   (B) Most of the people are playing baseball.
      ほとんどの人が、野球をしている。
   (C) The park is pretty crowded.
      遊園地は、かなり混雑している。
   (D) The park is located inside a large building.
      遊園地は、大きなビルの中にある。

正解：**(C)**
解説：(A) look toward「～のほうを見る」。(B) most of「～のほとんど」。(C) pretty crowded「かなり混雑した」。(D) inside「～の中に」。

Part 2

3. You might want to try on this kimono.
    この着物を試着してみてはいかがですか？
    (A) It will be better that way.　そうしたほうがいいでしょう。
    (B) You were right.　あなたの言ったとおりでした。
    (C) OK, I think I will.　はい、そうしてみます。

    正解：**(C)**
    解説：might want to は、「～するといいかもしれない」という控えめな提案。(C)「そうしてみます」と応えている (C) が正解。

4. How do you handle inquiries?
    質問に、どのように対応していますか？
    (A) I don't see any handles.　ハンドルなんて見えません。
    (B) I'll show you.　説明しましょう。
    (C) Not very often.　それほど頻繁ではありません。

    正解：**(B)**
    解説：How で始まる問いかけ文は、「方法」を尋ねる疑問文。handle inquiries は、「質問に対応する」。「説明しましょう」と応えている (B) が正解。

5. Are you expected to attend the dinner tonight?
    今夜のディナーに招待されていますか？
    (A) Yes, I'm expecting it.　はい、それを期待しています。
    (B) I am. How about you?　はい。あなたは？
    (C) I think I'll skip dinner tonight, thanks.
    　　今夜は、夕食を抜こうと思っています、どうも。

    正解：**(B)**
    解説：Are you expected to + 動詞？ は、「～することを期待されているか？」。Are you に対し、I am と応答している (B) が正解。

Part 3

放送文

Questions 6–8 refer to the following conversation.

M: Where did I put those staples? I just bought a new box yesterday. Where could they have gotten to? I was sure I put them in this desk drawer somewhere. Or maybe I left them in my briefcase...No, not in there.
W: Barry, are you looking for these? I borrowed them this morning. Sorry, I forgot to leave a note on the desk there for you...
M: Next time, please do. It drives me crazy looking for stuff in my desk.
W: I know the feeling. Sorry about that. I'll remember next time.

問題 6–8 は、次の会話に関するものです。
M: ホッチキスの針をどこに置いたっけ？　昨日新しいのを１箱買ったばかりだけれど。どこにいったかなあ？　確かにこの机の引出しのどこかに入れたのだけれど。それともブリーフケースに入れたままかも……いや、その中にはない。
W: バリー、これを探しているの？　今朝借りたの。ごめんなさい、机の上にあなたにメモを置いておくのを忘れたわ。
M: 次回は、頼むよ。自分の机のものを探すのはいらだつんだよ。
W: その気持ちわかるわ。ごめんなさいね。今度は忘れないようにする。

語句

staple：ホッチキスの針
get to：〜に行く
briefcase：書類カバン
borrow：〜を借りる
drive me crazy：〜にいらだつ

could：[可能] 〜なんてことがありうるのか
drawer：引出し
forget to + 動詞：〜し忘れる
please do：ぜひ、そうしてください
stuff：（漠然と）物

設問

6. 会話の初めで、男性の口調はどうですか？
   (A) 混乱した
   (B) わかりにくい
   (C) 興奮した
   (D) エキサイティングな

   正解：**(A)**
   ヒント：Where could they have gotten to?

7. 女性は、何をし忘れましたか？
   (A) 自分のホッチキスを買うこと
   (B) 何かを借りたことを男性に知らせること
   (C) バリーが机の上に置いたメモを読むこと
   (D) 男性の机の引出しを閉めること

   正解：**(B)**
   ヒント：I forgot to leave a note on the desk there for you…

8. 会話の終わりで、女性は何をすることに同意しますか？
   (A) 男性の机の上を整頓する
   (B) 男性のホッチキスの針を返す
   (C) 彼女が間違いをしたときに謝罪する
   (D) コミュニケーションをよりよくする

   正解：**(D)**
   ヒント：男性の Next time, please do. と、女性の I'll remember next time.

Part 4

放送文

Questions 9–11 refer to the following advertisement.
Why bank with United Mutual? Is free checking and free online banking / not enough to get you to switch? How about a $100 gift card / from O'Shea's, Home Decorators or Swiss Sports, if you switch / anytime before December 31st of this year? If that doesn't convince you, this will: / We're open till 8 p.m. / Thursdays and Fridays. That's right! We don't believe in "banker's hours" / anymore than you do. So drop in / when it's convenient for you / and talk to any of our banking representatives / about switching. United Mutual—the way banking should be.

問題 9–11 は、次の広告に関するものです。
(※日本語訳は、英語の原文の順序どおりに記してあります。)
なぜユナイテッド・ミューチュアルに口座を持つのかですって？　無料当座預金と無料オンライン取引では / 切り替えるのに十分ではないのですか？　ギフトカード 100 ドル分ではどうですか / オシアかホーム・デコレーターズかスイス・スポーツの、お切り替えになれば / 今年の 12 月 31 日以前に？　それでも納得がいただけないのなら、これでどうですか / 当行は夜 8 時まで営業しています / 木曜と金曜は。そうです！　当行は「銀行時間」など認めません / お客様と同様に。ですからお立ち寄りください / あなたのご都合のいい時に / そして、当行の担当者にご相談ください / 切り替えについて。ユナイテッド・ミューチュアルは、銀行業務のあるべき姿です。

語句

bank with：〜銀行に預金する
switch：切り替える
this will のあとに convince you が省略
"banker's hours"：3 時閉店の伝統的な銀行
anymore than you do：[否定文で] あなた以上に〜しない
drop in：立ち寄る
checking：当座預金
convince：〜を説得する
believe in：〜を信じている
the way 〜 should be：〜の本来あるべき姿

設問

9. ユナイテッド・ミューチュアルのセールスポイントの1つは、何ですか？
    (A) すべてのサービスが安い
    (B) 便利な所在地
    (C) 長い営業時間
    (D) 適正料金でのプロのアドバイス

    正解：**(C)**
    ヒント：We're open till 8 p.m. Thursdays and Fridays.

10. 1月2日にユナイテッド・ミューチュアルに切り替えた人は、何を逃しますか？
    (A) 午後8時までの銀行業務
    (B) プレゼント
    (C) 無料の当座預金
    (D) 無料のオンライン・バンキング

    正解：**(B)**
    ヒント：How about a $100 gift card from O'Shea's, Home Decorators or Swiss Sports, if you switch anytime before December 31st of this year?

11. 広告をもっともよく表わしているのは、次のどれですか？
    (A) 12月31日以降に会社で予定されている変革の概要
    (B) ユナイテッド・ミューチュアルの略歴
    (C) 無料の当座預金とオンライン・バンキングについての説明
    (D) 銀行を利用することの利点の一覧

    正解：**(D)**
    ヒント：全体の内容から判断。

Part 5

12. 洗濯物を調べて、ポーラは色が落ちているのに気づいた。

    正解：**(A)**
    解説：found（過去形）した内容（that 以下）が起こったのは found した時点より前なので、had run（過去完了形）を選ぶ。run は、「（色など）が落ちる」。時制変化：find-found-found, run-run-run
    例文：Paula found that the colors had run.
    ポーラは色が落ちているのに気づいた。

13. さらに悪いことに、彼らは来週まで何もできない。

    正解：**(B)**
    解説：文意から、慣用句 to make matters worse「さらに悪いことに」を完成させる。
    例文：To make matters worse, they cannot do anything now.
    さらに悪いことに、彼らは今何もできない。

14. その会社は、明後日電気システムの改良作業を行なうが、すべての部署は業務を続けるだろう。

    正解：**(B)**
    解説：文意から、後半の節の内容と反する前半の節を結ぶ接続詞 Even though「〜だとしても」を選ぶ。remain は、「〜の（状態の）ままである」。(A)「まるで〜のように」（接続詞）、(C)「それゆえに」（副詞）、(D)「〜内に」（前置詞）。
    例文：Even though the building is being repaired, all offices will remain open.
    ビルが修理中でも、すべてのオフィスは業務を続けるだろう。

Part 6

問題 15–17 は次の招待状に関するものです。

> ゲイリー・ウィリスがユニオン市の財務長官を辞職すると発表したわずか1週間後に、3名が立候補を表明しています。最後に立候補したのは、在任3年の現職副財務長官マーシャ・フリーマンです。副財務長官として、彼女は納税案内と未納税の徴収を主に担当してきました。また、過去2年間、州財政の監査報告書の編纂も行なっています。

15. 正解：**(B)**
    解説：文意から、seek を選び、seek the office「官職をめざす」を完成させる。office「官職」。
    例文：Three people have said they will seek the office.
    3名が官職への立候補を表明しています。

16. 正解：**(A)**
    解説：for three years「3年間」から、現在完了形 has held を選ぶ。(D) は、has been holding なら可。
    例文：It is an office she has held for three years.
    それは、彼女が3年間在職している官職です。

17. 正解：**(D)**
    解説：形容詞 responsible を修飾する副詞 chiefly「主として」を選ぶ。be responsible for「〜に責任がある」。
    例文：She has been chiefly responsible for tax billing.
    彼女は主として納税案内を担当してきました。

Part 7（読解問題-シングルパッセージ）

問題 18-20 は次の広告に関するものです。

ローレライで作る身体
働く女性のためのスキンケア・システム

ボトックス
わずか数回の少量の注射で眉間のしわを取り除きます。数日で違いを実感されるでしょう。施術の効果は最長で3カ月持続します。
注射1回につき15ドル

マッサージ・セラピー
あなたに必要なマッサージを判断する全身のコンサルテーションのあと、当店の経験豊富なプロのマッサージ・セラピストがあなたの身体のあらゆる痛みを和らげる施術をいたします。
30分：70ドル　60分：110ドル　90分：150ドル

マイクロ皮膚剥離術
傷んで老廃物となった皮膚を取り除く最良の方法です。皮膚全体から細かい結晶を吸引し、皮膚の深層組織を若返らせます。
背中：170ドル　首：35ドル　顔：150ドル　両肩：35ドル　両手：80ドル

スキンケア
当店のスキンケアのプロによるカスタム・メードの処置は、当店独自のボディマッピング技術に基づいています。これにより、当店では、あなたの問題のある部分に集中し、あなた専用の処置を設計することが可能です。
顔：120ドル　両手と両腕：80ドル　頭皮マッサージ：50ドル
両脚：70ドル　首と両肩：100ドル

語句	frown line：眉間のしわ injection：注射 rejuvenate：若返らせる zero in on：～に焦点を合わせる	tiny：わずかな量の soothe：和らげる skin tissue：皮膚組織

18. 筋肉痛の人が受けると思われるのは、どれですか？
    (A) スキンケア　　　　　　　(B) ボトックス
    (C) マイクロ皮膚剥離術　　　(D) マッサージ・セラピー
    正解：**(D)**
    ヒント：Massage Therapy の詳細、massage therapists go to work to soothe and treat all your aches and pains.

19. 特に個人別に設計されていると広告されているのは、どの処置ですか？
    (A) スキンケアとボトックス
    (B) マッサージ・セラピーとスキンケア
    (C) スキンケアとマイクロ皮膚剥離術
    (D) マイクロ皮膚剥離術とボトックス
    正解：**(B)**
    ヒント：Massage Therapy の詳細、After a total body consultation to determine your massage needs と、Skin Care の詳細、custom design your treatment.

20. 次の記述のうち、正しいものはどれですか？
    (A) マイクロ皮膚剥離術とスキンケアは身体の部位によって請求される。
    (B) マッサージ・セラピーとスキンケアは時間によって請求される。
    (C) ボトックスとマイクロ皮膚剥離術は注射の数によって請求される。
    (D) マッサージ・セラピーとボトックスは薬によって請求される。
    正解：**(A)**
    ヒント：Microdermabrasion の料金、Back: $170～ と、Skin Care の料金、Facials: $120～

Part 7（読解問題－ダブルパッセージ）

問題 21–25 は、次の記事と E メールに関するものです。

あなたの車はあなたを表わす
アダム・バーナード

人びとがどんな乗用車やトラックを運転しているかを見て、いろいろな想像をすることがよくあります。これは固定観念かもしれませんが、『ホィールズ』誌の調査は、「運転する車は身体を表わす」ことを証明しています。圧倒的に、大馬力の車やハマーの所有者は一般的に独身男性で、独身女性はスポーティーだが信頼性の高い小型車を好む傾向にありました。スポーツクーペの運転者は中年で、既婚者より独身男性が多いのです。子供のいる夫婦で車を 2 台持つ世帯は、典型的な SUV かミニバンを所有する傾向がありますが、2 台目についてはさまざまです。過半数がファミリーセダンを所有していましたが、堅実な 22 パーセントが 2 台目としてスポーツクーペを所有していました。この調査についてもっと詳しく知りたい方は、当社のウェブサイトで私のブログをクリックするか、お近くの新聞売店で『ホィールズ』誌最新版をお求めください。

アダム様

車が人の個性を反映するという記事に大変興味を持ちました。まったくそのとおりだと思います。私の親友サイモンは、結婚して 3 人の子持ちですが、まだムスタングへの愛着を捨てることができません。数年前にメーカーがムスタングの生産を再開した時、彼は真っ先に購入した 1 人でした。彼が中年の危機の真っ直中にいると言っているわけではありませんが、よりスポーツタイプのこの車を買うために、4 ドアのファミリーセダンを下取りに出したのです。

ウォルター・ロルフ（テキサス州ニューボストン）

語句	**stereotyping**：固定観念 "**we are what we drive**"：「乗っている車で、その人となりがわかる」 **overwhelmingly**：圧倒的に　　　　　**prefer**：より〜を好む **reliable**：信頼できる　　　　　　　　**range widely**：多種多様で **solid**：堅実な

21. この批評は、ドライバーに関するどんな固定観念に言及していますか？
    (A) 男性は、女性より運転が優れている。
    (B) どんな車に乗るかは、収入で決まる。
    (C) 車が、人びとの個性のヒントになる。
    (D) 年齢の高い人より、若い人のほうが事故が多い。

    正答：**(C)**
    ヒント：上段の文章の but a survey by Wheels magazine proves that "we are what we drive."

22. 最近車を購入したのは、誰ですか？
    (A) ウォルター・ロルフ
    (B) 批評に述べられた誰か
    (C) アダム・バーナード
    (D) E メールに述べられた人

    正答：**(D)**
    ヒント：下段の文章の he was one of the first to buy

23. E メールの差出人は、批評家の意見をどう考えていますか？
    (A) いくつか疑問点がある。
    (B) 批判している。
    (C) 支持している。
    (D) 何点か質問がある。

    正答：**(C)**

ヒント：下段の文の Couldn't agree more.

24. 調査によると、もっともスポーツカーを所有すると思われるのは誰ですか？
    (A) トム 29 歳
    (B) リサ 38 歳
    (C) ジャック 46 歳
    (D) ナンシーとフィル、どちらも 28 歳

    正答：**(C)**
    ヒント：上段の文の Sports coupes tended to be driven by more middle-aged men

25. 『ホィールズ』誌の調査についての情報をもっと得る方法は、何通りですか？
    (A) 1 通り   (B) 2 通り
    (C) 3 通り   (D) 4 通り

    正答：**(B)**
    ヒント：上段の文の If you want to learn more about the survey, go to our Web site and click on my blog or pick up the latest edition of Wheels at your newsstand.

＜ワンポイント＞

　ダブルパッセージの問題は、2つの英文を読んで、5つの設問に答えることが求められます。でも、焦る必要はありません。前述のとおり、600点突破には、**勘も含めて45％（20問中9問）の正答**で十分です。4セット（各5問）の中から比較的やさしそうな問題をまずチェックして、各英文の最初の数行を読み、**それぞれ何のために書かれた英文か**を把握します。これで、設問を読んだ際に、**どちらの英文から答えを探すように読めばよいのか**がわかります。比較的やさしい問題であれば、5分で1セット（5問）が解けます。最後まで、あきらめずにがんばりましょう！

本書の第 2 章〜第 5 章は、学習者向け英字新聞『週刊 ST』（ジャパンタイムズ）に、2002 年 4 月〜2010 年 3 月までの 8 年間（400 回）にわたって掲載された「TOEIC® テスト 実践トレーニング」の練習問題に加筆したものです。

●編集協力
　杉山まどか

●社内協力
　高見沢紀子・菅田晶子・小倉宏子・吉井瑠里・宮内繭子

●CD製作協力
　Peter Serafin and Xanthe Smith(Golden Angel Studio)[「語句」「指示文」ほかナレーション]
　吉田美穂(俳協)[「語句」日本語ナレーション]
　佐藤京子(東京録音)

● 著者紹介

http://www.icconsul.com/

鹿野　晴夫（かの　はるお）

1964 年北海道生まれ。東京都立大学工学部卒。現在、英語トレーニングの ICC 東京本校責任者。英語レベル別指導法のエキスパートとして、企業・大学で「英語トレーニング法」の講演・セミナーを多数担当するほか、英語教員向けに「英語トレーニングの指導法セミナー」を担当している。著書に、自らの学習経験を綴った「TOEIC®テスト 300 点から 800 点になる学習法」「TOEIC®テスト 900 点を突破する集中トレーニング」（以上、中経出版）をはじめとする TOEIC®テスト関連の著作が 40 点以上。2010 年には、『TOEIC®テスト　スピーキング／ライティング問題集』（研究社、千田潤一と共著）も刊行。

TOEIC®テスト　これだけ　直前1カ月　600点クリア

初版発行	2011 年 4 月 28 日
著者	鹿野晴夫 Copyright © 2011 by ICC
発行者	関戸雅男
発行	株式会社　研究社 〒102-8152　東京都千代田区富士見 2-11-3 電話　営業 03(3288)7777(代)　編集 03(3288)7711(代) 振替　00150-9-26710 http://www.kenkyusha.co.jp
印刷所	研究社印刷株式会社

KENKYUSHA
〈検印省略〉

＊

装丁・CD デザイン	久保和正
本文レイアウト・組版	(株)インフォルム
CD 編集・製作	(株)東京録音

ISBN978-4-327-43071-9 C1082

本書の全部または一部を無断で複写複製（コピー）することは、著作権法上での例外を除き禁じられています。
価格はカバーに表示してあります。

研究社の出版案内

鹿野晴夫〔著〕

TOEIC® テスト これだけ 直前1カ月 350点クリア

直前1カ月は、これだけきっちり仕上げよう！

英語が超苦手な方も、1カ月でTOEIC®の問題形式がわかる！

A5判 並製 184頁
ISBN 978-4-327-43069-6 C1082

CD付き

TOEIC® テスト これだけ 直前1カ月 470点クリア

英語力をのばしたい！
1カ月で確実にTOEIC®のスコアがアップ！

A5判 並製 184頁
ISBN 978-4-327-43070-2 C1082

CD付き

- ▶ TOEIC®テストのスコアを上げたい。
- ▶ でも、あまり時間がない。
- ▶ 通勤・通学の時間を有効に使いたい。

そんなみなさんのために、TOEIC®の問題形式に慣れるだけでなく、基本的な英語力のアップがはかれるように工夫しました。
『週刊ST』の人気コラムに大幅加筆して単行本化！

出版社による初のTOEIC® SWテスト実戦問題集！

TOEIC® テスト スピーキング／ライティング問題集

千田潤一・鹿野晴夫〔著〕

A5判 並製 180頁
ISBN 978-4-327-43068-9 C1082

CD付き